Integrating Academics

WORKBOOK

Prepared
by

CECIL H. NEILL
Jefferson County Public Schools
Louisville, KY

West Publishing Company

Minneapolis/St. Paul   Mew York   Los Angeles   San Francisco

WEST'S COMMITMENT TO THE ENVIRONMENT

In 1906, West Publishing Company began recycling materials left over from the production of books. This began a tradition of efficient and responsible use of resources. Today, 100% of our legal bound volumes are printed on acid-free, recycled paper consisting of 50% new paper pulp and 50% paper that has undergone a de-inking process. We also use vegetable-based inks to print all of our books. West recycles nearly 27,700,000 pounds of scrap paper annually—the equivalent of 229,300 trees. Since the 1960s, West has devised ways to capture and recycle waste inks, solvents, oils, and vapors created in the printing process. We also recycle plastics of all kinds, wood, glass, corrugated cardboard, and batteries, and have eliminated the use of polystyrene book packaging. We at West are proud of the longevity and the scope of our commitment to the environment.

West pocket parts and advance sheets are printed on recyclable paper and can be collected and recycled with newspapers. Staples do not have to be removed. Bound volumes can be recycled after removing the cover.

Production, Prepress, Printing and Binding by West Publishing Company.

 *TEXT IS PRINTED ON 10% POST CONSUMER RECYCLED PAPER*

COPYRIGHT © 1997 by WEST PUBLISHING CO.
610 Opperman Drive
P.O. Box 64526
St. Paul, MN 55164–0526

ISBN 0–314–09789–9

Table of Contents

Page

I Personal and Family Relationships

Environment 1
Heredity 3
Personality 4
Heroes 5
Study Time 6
Time Flies 7
No Smoking 8
Exercise and Health 9
Managing Stress 10
Editorial Page 13
Traditions 14
You and Your Family 15
Changes 16
Family Feuds 17
Roles 18
Dear Andy 19
Getting to Know You 20
Friends 21
Wedding Customs 22
Contracts 24
Children With Special Needs 25
Safety in the Home 26
Parenting Cost 27
Movie Reviews 28
Aging Vocabulary 29
Senior Services 31

II Consumer Matters

Budgeting 33
Your Paycheck 35
Making Money 37
Class Trip 38
Running a Business 39
Money Matters 40
Consumer Complaints 41
Buyer Beware! 42
Unit Pricing 44
Sales For Sale 45

Page

Senior $ Cost 46
Catalog Shopping 47

III Food and Nutrition

Carbohydrates/Fats 48
Vitamins 49
Nutrition Scoreboard 50
Food Pyramids 51
Water 52
Retaining Vitamins 53
Calories 54
Snacking 55
Student Preferences 56
Planning a Party 57
Breads Around the World 58
Grocery Shopping 60
Kitchen Tools 62
Suspensions and Emulsions 63
Safety and Sanitation 64
Osmosis 65
Let's Make Macaroni and Cheese 66
Measuring Volume 67
Let's Make Cookies 68
Sourdough 69
Leavening Agents 70
Lasagna 71
Herbs 72
Ripening Fruit 73
Recycling Food 74
Air As Leavening 75
Coagulation 76
Food Tips 77
Microwave Cooking 78
Evaporation 79
Extracts 80
Pretzel Play 81
Native American Foods 82
Ethnic Food Fair 83
Table Setting 84
Etiquette Review 85

Table of Contents

Page

IV Clothing

Clothing Classics 87
Fads 88
A Spending Plan 89
Sewing 90
Determining Clothing Cost 91
Designer Jeans: What's the Difference? 92
Threading the Machine 93
Special Occasion Clothing 94
Recycling 96
Clothing Construction 97

V Housing

Floor Covering 98
Wallpapering 99
Location 100
Floor Plans 101
Renting Apartments 102
Buying a House 104
On Your Own 105
Saving Electricity 106
Marriage Success 107
Help Wanted 108
Thank You 109
Volunteering 110
Career Choices 111
Your Résumé 112
Careers in Housing 113
Real Estate Terminology 114

Answers 115

Integrating Academics

Environment

Our personality is formed by the events and situations in our environment in combination with our heredity. Most of us cannot imagine being another person. When we read or watch a movie about people in other cultures, we begin to understand how each of us comes to be a unique individual. What kind of a person would you be if you were born into the following environments? Answer both questions with complete sentences.

1. Would your environment limit or increase your opportunities?

2. Would your environment mold your personality so that you would be a different person?

A. Raji: The child of a merchant in a small town in India.

   1. _____
   _____

   2. _____
   _____

B. Terry: The child of the President of the United States.

   1. _____
   _____

   2. _____
   _____

C. Toki: The child of a Japanese farmer in a small village.

   1. _____
   _____

   2. _____
   _____

Social Studies

1

Continued on next page

D. Amu: An Eskimo living in the frozen regions of Alaska.

1. _____

_____

2. _____

_____

E. Chris: The child of a famous Hollywood actor.

1. _____

_____

2. _____

_____

Name _____ Date _____ Period _____

Integrating Academics

Heredity

We inherit our physical and mental characteristics from our families. Has anyone ever said, "you look just like your mother?" Perhaps you don't think you look anything like your family. Many traits skip generations—you may resemble your great uncle Charlie! The following is a list of traits that are inherited. Indicate beside each one from whom you inherited the characteristic. **Example:** mother, father, other relative.

Blood type: _____

Hair color: _____

Eye color: _____

Shape of nose: _____

Height: _____

Right- or left-handedness: _____

Curly or straight hair: _____

Foot size: _____

Body shape: _____

Skin color: _____

Chin shape: _____

Do you have any ability or talent which you inherited? (**Example:** music, art, math or athletic skills.)

_____

_____

_____

_____

_____

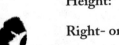

Science

Name _____ Date _____ Period _____

Integrating Academics

Personality

Most of us "like" people for various reasons. Maybe we think they are nice, fun to be with, or we just feel good when we are around them. We call these traits *personality*. We judge these personality traits or behaviors as either positive or negative. **Example:** friendliness would be a positive trait, selfishness would be a negative trait.

I. List in the columns below ten traits you would classify as positive and ten traits you would classify as negative.

Positive Personality Traits	**Negative Personality Traits**
1. _____	1. _____
2. _____	2. _____
3. _____	3. _____
4. _____	4. _____
5. _____	5. _____
6. _____	6. _____
7. _____	7. _____
8. _____	8. _____
9. _____	9. _____
10. _____	10. _____

II. Choose one of the positive traits you have listed and write a paragraph explaining how a person might acquire that trait.

_____

_____

_____

_____

4

Social Studies

Integrating Academics

Heroes

Children in the past easily identified persons they considered to be heroes. These heroes were admired for their nobility, courage, or exploits. They were looked upon by children growing up as people they would like to imitate. The amount of publicity that public figures receive today makes it hard to find heroes. Perhaps there is someone whom you admire who is not a public figure. Who would you choose to be like among the people you know today? Choose one person, and write a short essay explaining why you admire that person and why he or she is a "hero" to you.

My Hero

_____

_____

_____

_____

_____

_____

_____

_____

_____

_____

_____

_____

_____

_____

_____

_____

_____

_____

Language Arts

Integrating Academics

Study Time

Just as each of us has a different way of playing or working, so we all have different ways of studying. However, if we wish to be successful in our school work, studying is important. People who spend time determining how a person learns best have set some guidelines for making study time as productive as possible. Go to the library and read about the best way to use your time when studying. Produce a phamplet of "Dos and Don'ts" to share with a younger student.

Sudying Dos	Studying Don'ts

Language Arts

Name _____ Date _____ Period _____

Integrating Academics

Time Flies

What does your typical week look like? How do you spend your time? Your list probably includes school, chores, visiting with friends, eating, sleeping, watching TV, and homework. Have you ever thought about how much time you spend doing these things? Is there any time left over ? If you are involved in extra activities at school or church, you may not have enough time to do everything you would like to. A good method of time management is to figure out where you are spending your time, and then you can determine if there are any wasted hours that could be used to do some new things you might like to try.

1. List below the main things you spend your time on in a typical *week*. Estimate beside each activity the amount of time you spend on that activity in the week.

Activity	**Time Spent**
a. _____	_____
b. _____	_____
c. _____	_____
d. _____	_____
e. _____	_____
f. _____	_____

2. In the space below, draw a circle graph to show how your time is divided. Label each segment.

3. Do you see any changes you would like to make? _____

7

Math

Integrating Academics

No Smoking

Citing an alarming rise in pre-teen and teenage smoking, government officials have begun to formulate more effective ways to enforce a current law which forbids the sale of cigarettes to anyone under the age of eighteen. One recent development has been to recruit Youth Ambassadors from the "Smoke-Free Class of 2000." If you were a member of Youth Ambassadors, what three things would you tell other teenagers about the dangers of smoking?

1. _____

2. _____

3. _____

Write a paragraph explaining each of the three points you wish to make. You may use examples from your personal experience or consult your textbook.

_____

_____

_____

_____

_____

_____

_____

_____

_____

_____

_____

_____

_____

Language Arts

Integrating Academics

Exercise and Health

A healthy lifestyle is defined as eating nutritious foods and getting the right amount of exercise for your age, weight, and sex. The benefits of these two recommendations are important in the prevention of illness and the enhancement of overall health. You will look better, your mood will be elevated, you will have more energy and you will sleep better. The recommended frequency of exercise is a minimum of three times a week for twenty to thirty continuous minutes. To achieve the maximum cardiorespiratory effects you should work at 70 to 85% of your **Maximum Heart Rate**.

I. To calculate your maximum heart rate:

1. 220 minus your age in years = MHR

    If you are 17, your MHR = 203 beats per minute.

    Calculate your MHR 220 − _____ = _____ beats per minute.

2. Calculate target heart rate of 70 to 85% of MHR

    .70 × 203 = 142 beats per minute.

    .85 × 203 = 172 beats per minute. The example's range is between 142–172.

    Calculate your Target Heart Rate Range

    .70 × _____ = _____ beats per minute.

    .85 × _____ = _____ beats per minute.

    Your Target Heart Range is between _____ and _____.

II. The average heart rate is approximately 72 beats per minute. The rate varies from one individual to another. To determine your resting heart rate, you must take your pulse. Place your fingers on the thumb side of your wrist, at your temple, over your heart or at your carotid artery (between your Adam's apple and the large muscles on the side of your neck.) Use the second hand on a watch and count the number of beats for 60 seconds.

Begin your exercise activity. At the end of 10 minutes calculate your heart rate. Is it in your target range? Calculate again when finished.

Math

9

Integrating Academics

Managing Stress

Many factors contribute to stress in families.

1. Dramatic changes in technology have speeded up our workplace to such an extent that most Americans suffer from chronic fatigue.

2. Many single parents are trying to fill dual parenthood roles; two-parent families are likely to find both parents working outside the home.

3. Our society has become more dangerous with widespread use of drugs and guns.

When family members feel stressed, conflict arises. As a teenager, you have the choice of adding to that stress or seeking ways to help your family unit cope more efficiently.

Below are a variety of situations. List at least two ways you might help make them less stressful.

1. You want to go to a ballgame at seven o'clock and your mother does not get home to start dinner until six-thirty.

   a. _____

   b. _____

2. Your six-year-old brother has no clean clothes, and the bus is coming to take him to school in 15 minutes.

   a. _____

   b. _____

3. Your room has not been cleaned in three weeks and you have been told three times to do it; you will probably be grounded.

   a. _____

   b. _____

4. Report time comes and you bring home a "D" in math.

   a. _____

   b. _____

10 *Continued on next page*

Social Studies

5. No one fed the dog today, and your father is threatening to call the Humane Society.

   a. _____

   b. _____

6. You forgot to tell your mother you have to take cookies to school tomorrow.

   a. _____

   b. _____

7. The dishes from breakfast are still on the table and it is time to start dinner.

   a. _____

   b. _____

8. You and your friends ate the pie that your mother had baked for her club meeting.

   a. _____

   b. _____

9. You tore your new forty-seven dollar jeans playing football in the yard.

   a. _____

   b. _____

10. Your father has told the family he is being transferred.

    a. _____

    b. _____

11. Your mother did not get the promotion she had been counting on at work.

    a. _____

    b. _____

12. You have been told that there is no money for band camp.

    a. _____

    b. _____

11

Continued on next page

Compare some of your solutions with those of your friends. Did you learn any different ways to solve the same problems?

_____

_____

_____

_____

_____

_____

_____

Do you think that your attitude can make a bad situation better? Explain your answer.

_____

_____

_____

_____

_____

_____

_____

Integrating Academics

Editorial Page

Recent studies of juvenile crime have predicted that arrests for violent crimes may double by the year 2010. Youths under the age of eighteen are becoming known as the "young and ruthless." What is the solution to the problem of weapon-toting children? Many communities are suggesting that teen curfews may be an answer. What do you think? Editorials express the writer's opinion. In the space provided below, write an editorial about your views concerning teen curfews.

Teen Curfews

An editorial by _____

_____

_____

_____

_____

_____

_____

_____

_____

_____

_____

_____

_____

_____

_____

_____

_____

_____

Language Arts

Name _____ Date _____ Period _____

Integrating Academics

Traditions

Family traditions and customs are unique to each family unit. Some are handed down from parents and grandparents and are related to our cultural heritage; others just happen as members begin to expect certain foods or ways of celebrating events and a pattern emerges. (**Example:** Children might always expect to have their favorite foods on their birthdays.)

1. Write a paragraph identifying a family tradition or custom in your family. Explain how it developed.

    _____

    _____

    _____

    _____

    _____

2. What family traditions do you want to continue with your own family in the future?

    _____

    _____

    _____

    _____

    _____

3. Why do you think traditions are important in strengthing relationships within the family unit?

    _____

    _____

    _____

    _____

    _____

Social Studies

Integrating Academics

You and Your Family

Many situations arise that cause disagreements between teenagers and parents, especially in the areas of where you are going, with whom you are going, and what time you will be home. Create a dialogue between you and your mother or father which would relate a typical conversation at your house if the following situations occurred. Describe the sound of each voice with descriptive terms. **Example:** snapped, ordered, reminded, warned, etc.

1. **Situation:** You have been invited to go on a trip which will not be chaperoned during spring break with a group of friends.

   _____

   _____

   _____

   _____

2. **Situation:** Your counselor has called home to report that you were not at school today. You left home at the usual school time.

   _____

   _____

   _____

   _____

3. **Situation:** You want to spend the night with a friend whom your parents have not met.

   _____

   _____

   _____

   _____

Language Arts

Integrating Academics

Changes

Most American families move from one place to another several times in any one generation. These moves have different effects on each family member. It is especially difficult for teenagers to have to leave their friends and change schools. Find a person in your class who has moved from a small town to a city, from a farm to a town, or from a city to a small town. There may even be someone who has moved from one country to another. Interview that person to find out what problems they experienced, what good things resulted, and how they handled the stress.

In addition, ask the person to compare the place he or she grew up in to the place moved to in the following ways:

1) physical surroundings

2) general atmosphere

3) kind of people

4) experiences that were good

5) experiences that were bad

Write the interview as if you were writing a story for the school newspaper. Be sure to answer the questions, who, what, where, when and why.

Who _____

_____

What _____

_____

Where _____

_____

When _____

_____

Why _____

_____

Name _____ Date _____ Period _____

Integrating Academics

Family Feuds

Conflicts between family members usually occur when each person has expected something different from the other and at least one family member is disappointed. Most of these disagreements are usually settled with each person compromising to some degree. Sometimes the disagreement is allowed to worsen, and tempers flare. We read of many different situations which occur in family settings and of many different solutions to these conflicts. Look in a current magazine to find an account of how the families in the article handled the conflict described. Read the article and prepare a written summary to share with the class orally.

Magazine: _____

Author: _____

Title of article: _____

Summary: _____

_____

_____

_____

_____

_____

_____

_____

_____

Was this article a good example of conflict resolution? Why, or why not?

_____

_____

_____

_____

_____

17

Language Arts

Integrating Academics

Roles

I. Everyday we interact with many different people. Each time this happens we play a different part or role. Below are listed some roles which teenagers usually have to play. Beside each, write how you are expected to act in that role. (**Example:** Student—be respectful, industrious, and helpful in the classroom.)

Friend _____

Brother or sister _____

Team member _____

Child to parent _____

Worker _____

Classmate _____

Neighbor _____

Leader _____

Baby sitter _____

Driver _____

Grandchild _____

Aunt or uncle _____

II. Put a check mark by the role you like the most. Explain the reason you chose that role.

_____

_____

_____

_____

_____

Social Studies

Integrating Academics

Dear Andy

Many people write to advice columnists for help in handling personal and family problems. Read the letter below. Write an answer to Jennifer using the information you have learned in class about dating violence.

Nov. 20, 199_

Dear Andy,

I have a friend named Sarah whom I have known since elementary school. We are both fifteen now, and although we do not spend much time together, I still care about her. The reason we do not spend time together is that she is always with her boyfriend Steve. He never wants her to go anywhere with her girl friends, and she has to sit at home waiting for him to call. Monday she came to school with a really horrible black eye. I know that Steve hit her because he has done it before. Andy, she won't listen to me or anyone else. Can you tell me what I should do to help her before she gets hurt really badly?

Jennifer
Kansas

Language Arts

Dear Jennifer,

_____
_____
_____
_____
_____
_____
_____
_____
_____
_____
_____

Name _____ Date _____ Period _____

Integrating Academics

Getting to Know You

Making really good friends can take a long time. It takes many shared experiences both good and bad to get to know someone well. How well do you know yourself? What are your likes and dislikes? How do you react to disappointment or joy? Fill in the blanks below to make a complete sentence.

1. My favorite color is _____.

2. The sport I like best is _____.

3. When I get mad I _____.

4. My most embarrassing time was _____.

5. My career goals are _____.

6. My favorite subject in school is _____.

7. When I get excited I _____.

8. I like people who _____.

9. I am happiest when _____.

10. Picture yourself 50 years from now listening to your grandchildren talk about you. What would you like to hear them say?

_____

_____

_____

_____

_____

_____

_____

_____

Language Arts

Name _____ Date _____ Period _____

Integrating Academics

Friends

The social changes experienced by teenagers are most evident in how important the peer group becomes at this time of life. Relationships between adolescent friends become significantly more important and the teen prefers to spend time with friends rather than family. Many friendships begun during this time last for a lifetime. Enduring friendships all have similar qualities. Read about the qualities of friendship in your textbook.

Think of who your best friends are. Can you describe those qualities about them that make them special to you?

Draw a word picture to describe your friends.

Example: E — Empathetic
R — Reliable
I — Interesting
C — Caring

Friend Number One   **Friend Number Two**

_____   _____

_____   _____

_____   _____

_____   _____

_____   _____

_____   _____

Draw a word picture to describe yourself. Is the same picture drawn by your friend?

Me   **Me (as seen by a friend)**

_____   _____

_____   _____

_____   _____

_____   _____

21

Language Arts

Name _____ Date _____ Period _____

Integrating Academics

Wedding Customs

Traditional and non-traditional wedding ceremonies are generally similar in both words and actions. These words and actions are called customs. Many wedding customs originated in other countries and in different religions, and have existed since ancient times. Many brides and grooms are unaware of the original meaning of the symbolism expressed in these customary parts of the ceremony. Look in the library for the original meaning of the following customs:

Example: Why is rice thrown at the newlyweds?

Rice is the grain of the harvest and was a symbol of fertility. Throwing rice was a way of wishing the bride and groom many children!

1. Why is the wedding ring worn on the left hand?

_____

_____

2. Why does the father give the bride away?

_____

_____

3. What does lighting candles mean?

_____

_____

4. Why does grooms have a best man?

_____

_____

5. Why does the bride wear a bridal veil?

_____

_____

Continued on next page

Social Studies

6. What does carrying the bride over the threshold symbolize?

_____

_____

7. Why is a wedding trip called a honeymoon?

_____

_____

Which of these customs would you include in your wedding if you were to get married?

_____

_____

_____

_____

_____

_____

Name _____ Date _____ Period _____

Integrating Academics

Contracts

Marriage between two people is really a legal contract. Unlike what happens in the business world, the marriage contract is seldom written, and expectations are not documented. If a couple has not communicated those expectations to each other, relationships suffer, and many marriages do not survive. Below are listed common areas of conflict in marriage. Write a paragraph explaining what you would expect from your spouse if you were married.

1. Lifestyles: _____

2. Having and raising children: _____

3. Making and handling money: _____

4. Relationships with in-laws: _____

5. Use of leisure time: _____

6. Acceptable housing options: _____

7. Housework responsibilities: _____

8. Showing affection and intimacy: _____

9. Relationships with friends: _____

10. Compromising on food choices: _____

If you are in an exclusive relationship, it would be helpful to discuss these topics after you have written down your expectations. If you have disagreements, can you compromise? What are some other important topics which should be examined?

_____

_____

_____

_____

_____

_____

Language Arts

Integrating Academics

Children With Special Needs

Technology is helping all people with disabilities to lead more normal lives. Children with a special need who are born today can communicate at very early ages through the new technology. Look in the library for examples of inventions which aid the disabled. Write a summary explaining how each works. Plan a field trip to a school in your area which has classes for children with special needs.

1. TDD (Telecommunications Device for the Deaf)

   _____

   _____

2. ERICA (Eyeglaze Response Interface Computer Aid)

   _____

   _____

3. Braille Writer

   _____

   _____

4. Other: _____

   _____

   _____

5. Other: _____

   _____

   _____

6. Other: _____

   _____

   _____

Language Arts

Integrating Academics

Safety in the Home

When the fire alarm rings in the school building each person knows the procedure for safely exiting the building. If the smoke alarm went off at your house and you woke up to a fire, would you know the safe way to exit your house? Would all the family members know what safety measures should be followed? Thinking about the escape routes, can you design a family fire safety procedure? If there are small children, who will see to their safe exit? If there is anyone with a physical disability, who will be responsible for him or her? In the space provided below, draw an escape route for your family in case of fire. Show the plan to your family and discuss any other ways to handle a fire emergency.

Escape Route

Social Studies

Integrating Academics

Parenting Cost

Parenting means to take care of your children's physical, social, mental, and emotional needs so that they are able to grow into healthy, well adjusted adults. Read the chapter in your textbook about the responsibilities of parenthood. Summarize the qualities necessary to fulfill these needs.

Physical Needs: _____

_____

_____

Social Needs: _____

_____

_____

Mental Needs: _____

_____

_____

Emotional Needs: _____

_____

_____

Each of these areas requires resources of time and money. Explain.

_____

_____

_____

_____

_____

_____

_____

Social Studies

Integrating Academics

Movie Reviews

Parents are urged to supervise the movies that their children watch. Many sociologists cite the viewing of violent films as a factor in the rise of violent crime in America. We know that educators have long used films and videos as teaching tools, so there is some agreement that we do learn from what we watch. One way that parents can choose acceptable films for their children to view is to read the movie reviews. Movie reviews are written to persuade a reader that a movie is worth, or is not worth, seeing. It gives enough information so that a person can draw a conclusion about whether they would, or would not, want to view the film. Select a recent film that you have seen that you feel would be appropriate for elementary school children to watch. Write a movie review for parents. If you have not seen a film which you think is appropriate for children, you may review one which you think is inappropriate.

Movie Reviewed: _____

_____

_____

_____

_____

_____

_____

_____

_____

_____

_____

_____

_____

_____

_____

_____

_____

Language Arts

Integrating Academics

Aging Vocabulary

Many terms which we read or hear daily refer to the older segment of our population. Young people are generally not familiar with these words.

Go to the library and research each of the terms listed below. Write a sentence or short paragraph describing each.

Medicare: _____

_____

_____

Medicaid: _____

_____

_____

Dementia: _____

_____

_____

Alzheimer's: _____

_____

_____

Assisted living: _____

_____

_____

Short-term memory loss: _____

_____

_____

Language Arts

Adult foster care: _____

_____

_____

Adult day programs: _____

_____

_____

Adaptive clothing: _____

_____

_____

Activity professionals: _____

_____

_____

Nursing home: _____

_____

_____

Geriatrics: _____

_____

_____

Visiting nurses: _____

_____

_____

Parkinson's: _____

_____

_____

Integrating Academics

Senior Services

Because of the growing number of aging people in America, businesses and institutions are establishing a variety of services designed to help older people stay independent and involved as long as their health permits. Nearly every family has someone who could benefit from these services. A partial list of services is provided below. Conduct a survey for the number and type of programs offered in your community. For each number, answer the following:

    a. Describe each by telling who funds the program

    b. Where it is carried out

    c. What services are offered

    d. Is there any cost to individuals enrolled

1. **Banking discounts:** _____

_____

_____

2. **Retired senior volunteer programs:** _____

_____

_____

3. **Senior citizen travel groups:** _____

_____

_____

4. **Restaurant and retail store discounts:** _____

_____

_____

5. **Day care programs:** _____

_____

_____

Social Studies

Continued on next page

6. Foster grandparent programs: _____

_____

_____

7. Time banks: _____

_____

_____

8. Meals on wheels: _____

_____

_____

9. Elderhostel: _____

_____

_____

10. Electric shopping carts: _____

_____

_____

11. Reverse mortgages: _____

_____

_____

Name _____ Date _____ Period _____

Integrating Academics

Budgeting

A **budget** is a plan for managing your money in the best way to be sure it stretches from one paycheck to the next, or from one week to the next if you are receiving an allowance. Every one has certain needs which have to be provided for. Probably your family is responsible for the most basic needs of food and shelter now. However, there are other wants which we have that vary from person to person. Most of us have to save for some of those things. That is how a budget can help! Below is a list of common items that you may have to set money aside for. Add to the list those things that you want or additional expenses that you may have. Beside each item, calculate the approximate amount of money required in a month.

Expenses	Monthly Costs
School lunches	$ _____
School supplies	_____
School club dues or fees	_____
Clothing items	_____
Snacks	_____
Transportation costs	_____
Entertainment	_____
Gifts	_____
Savings	_____
Others _____	_____
_____	_____
_____	_____
_____	_____
TOTAL	_____

Math

1. Will your income from jobs, family gifts, or allowances cover the amount needed?

    a. Yes _____

    b. No _____

2. Can you save at least 20% of your income for emergencies?

    a. Yes _____

    b. No _____

    Explain what areas, if any, you can adjust to save.

    _____

    _____

    _____

    _____

3. Many teenagers skip lunch to save money. Can you adjust other spending and still eat the lunch needed for energy and a healthy body?

    _____

    _____

    _____

    _____

    _____

    _____

    _____

    _____

    _____

    _____

    _____

Integrating Academics

Your Paycheck

Many young workers on their first job anxiously await their first paycheck. The hourly rate is agreed upon, the number of hours is set, and the expected reward of a week's work has been calculated. Then the check arrives and the amount is less than expected. When the accompanying pay stub is examined, the mystery is solved. The money subtracted from your wages is called **deductions**. Read the list of common deductions below and research what the money for taxes and other items is used for. Summarize your findings.

1. F.I.C.A—

_____

_____

_____

2. Federal Income Taxes—

_____

_____

_____

3. State Income Taxes—

_____

_____

_____

4. County Taxes—

_____

_____

_____

Language Arts

Continued on next page

5. City Taxes—

_____

_____

_____

6. Retirement Contribution—

_____

_____

_____

7. Union Dues—

_____

_____

_____

8. Savings Bond—

_____

_____

_____

Integrating Academics

Making Money

Many classrooms devise ways to make money for class projects or trips when funds are unavailable. Two examples are given below. Calculate the amount of money each class made. Show all your work so you can check your answer.

1. **Mrs. Smith's Class:** The class decided to buy 12 boxes of candy bars for $3.00 a box. Each box contained 12 bars and each candy bar was sold for $.75. How much profit did the class make?

Profit: _____

2. **Mr. Allen's Class:** The class bought six rolls of slice-and-bake cookies for $1.89 each. Each roll made 24 cookies after they were baked. They were able to sell all the cookies for $.25 each. How much money did they make?

Profit: _____

3. If the class needed to make $100.00 profit, how much of either product would they have to sell?

Candy: _____

Cookies: _____

37

Math

Name _____ Date _____ Period _____

Integrating Academics

Class Trip

I. The seventh-grade class at Butler Middle School is planning to take a trip to the amusement park at the end of the year. There are 120 class members so they will have to rent four school busses at $50.00 each. The tickets will be $28.00 each for the students and 12 adult chaperones. How much will the class have to raise for everyone to go?

II. What will the cost be for each person who decides to pay his or her own way (including $10.00 apiece for food)?

Math

Name _____ Date _____ Period _____

Integrating Academics

Running a Business

Babysitting is usually the first business transaction that many young teens experience. Those willing to become organized and dependable can build a profitable business, at the same time as they are gaining experience in managing their time and resources. If you think babysitting is a business you might want to explore, there are some things you need to learn before you start. Use your textbook, interview your friends who are already in the business, and talk to parents to find the answers to the following questions:

1. What is the hourly rate for sitting in your neighborhood? _____

2. Are there different hourly charges for families with more than one child? _____

3. Will you charge more for very late hours? _____ If yes, how much? _____

4. How will you be transported to your job?_____

5. Will you require references before you go into a strange house to sit?_____

6. Will you expect to be paid on the day or night you work? _____

7. Will you accept a check or would you prefer cash? _____

8. If you are forced to cancel in an emergency, will you be expected to find a replacement?

   _____

9. Will any extra work, like cleaning up the kitchen, be included in the hourly rate, or would

   you expect additional pay? _____

10. Will you need references from your first job to help you secure additional work? _____

Social Studies

Name _____ Date _____ Period _____

Integrating Academics

Money Matters

Perhaps Tevye in the play *Fiddler on the Roof* is the only one who has it figured out when he sings "If I Were a Rich Man." Many of us dream of winning the lottery, a 10 million dollar prize drawing, or a raffle at the school. We may have a list of "things to buy" or "places to go." How do you think suddenly having a large amount of money would change your life? Would it affect your family relationships?

Write a short essay in which you answer the question:

What Would I Do with a Million Dollars?

_____

_____

_____

_____

_____

_____

_____

_____

_____

_____

_____

_____

_____

_____

_____

Language Arts

Name _____   Date _____   Period _____

Integrating Academics

Consumer Complaints

If you have purchased an item which does not work correctly, has parts missing or was damaged in some way, you have the right as a consumer to have the item replaced or to receive a refund. Because some stores do not have the replacement merchandise or because the time for requesting a refund has expired, you may have to write to the manufacturer to file a complaint. A letter of this type is considered a business letter and the proper form should be followed, as shown below.

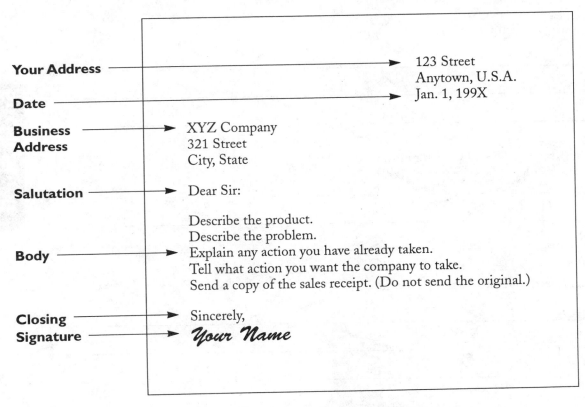

Your Address

123 Street
Anytown, U.S.A.

Date

Jan. 1, 199X

Business Address

XYZ Company
321 Street
City, State

Salutation

Dear Sir:

Body

Describe the product.
Describe the problem.
Explain any action you have already taken.
Tell what action you want the company to take.
Send a copy of the sales receipt. (Do not send the original.)

Closing

Sincerely,

Signature

Your Name

Language Arts

On a separate piece of paper write a letter of complaint. Be sure you include all the information necessary. Use correct punctuation, spelling, and capitalization.

Integrating Academics

Buyer Beware!

Most of us know about *impulse buying*, the purchases we come home with which we did not intend to buy! Experts tell us that the smart way to shop is to make a list and stick to it. However, it may be necessary to research a few of our purchases before they go on the list. We often see advertising for items that seem too good to be true. They probably are! From the list below, choose the products that you think would not be a good buy, and write a sentence to explain how you made that decision.

1. "Below manufacturer's cost!"

_____

_____

_____

2. "Comparable to $79.99 value for only $29.99"

_____

_____

_____

3. "Guaranteed to remove wrinkles overnight!"

_____

_____

_____

4. "New discovery cream melts fat away!"

_____

_____

_____

Social Studies

Continued on next page

5. "Our shoes will increase your leap by two feet!"

   _____

   _____

   _____

6. "Genuine gold plated necklace, $199.00"

   _____

   _____

   _____

7. "Guaranteed to win a Florida vacation, call today!"

   _____

   _____

   _____

Integrating Academics

Unit Pricing

To determine the best price of items being purchased, it is necessary to calculate the price per ounce, per pound, or by number of items per package. Once the unit price has been calculated, a decision can be made determining the best value. Most grocery items have the unit price listed on the store shelf under the item. If this is not the case, the unit price can easily be calculated. Divide the total price by the number of ounces etc.

Example: 16 oz. of spaghetti cost 69 cents, $69/16 = 4.31$ per ounce.

Calculate the unit price of the following items to determine the best buy:

1. a. 22 oz. cereal for $3.49   _____

   b. 14 oz cereal for $1.88   _____

      Best buy   _____

2. a. 1 qt. of milk for $ 1.04   _____

   b. 1 gallon of milk for $2.19   _____

      Best buy   _____

3. a. 1 lb. potatoes for $ .59   _____

   b. 5 lb. potatoes for $2.29   _____

      Best buy   _____

4. a. 13 oz. can of coffee for $2.79   _____

   b. 39 oz. can of coffee for $9.50   _____

      Best buy   _____

Math

Integrating Academics

Sales For Sale

Everyone loves a sale! Many shoppers search advertising supplements daily to determine the best buys for items on their shopping list. It may take some math skills to be able to figure out the exact discount for each purchase. Look at the methods of advertising discounts listed below. Calculate the percentage "off" for each unit purchased.

1. **Buy One Get One Free** _____%

   If you spend $10 on one shirt, and get the second one free, how much did each shirt actually cost? _____

2. **Buy One Regular Price, Second Item Half Off** _____%

   If you spend $40 on a pair of jeans, and get the second pair for half off, how much did you actually pay for each pair? _____

3. **Buy Three, Get Fourth Item Free** _____%

   If you buy three candy bars for $.60 each and receive a fourth candy bar free, how much did each candy bar cost? _____

4. **Buy Two, Get Third Item Free** _____%

   If you pay $3.00 each for two pairs of socks and get a third pair free, how much did each pair of socks cost? _____

Math

Name _____ Date _____ Period _____

Integrating Academics

Senior $ Cost

The excitement of arriving at the final moment of graduation has often been a stressful experience for teens who have not planned for the senior year expenses in advance. It is a good idea to begin calculating the cost early so that you can be financially prepared to meet those costs that you feel are important. Start by interviewing your friends who are already seniors, talk to the class advisors and school counselors, and make some telephone calls to begin comparison shopping. Below are listed some of the usual expenses. Research until you can assign a reasonable $ amount to each.

Expenses	Cost
Senior trips	
Class rings	
Graduation announcements	
Thank-you notes	
Cap and gown	
Mugs, sweatshirts, etc.	
Prom tickets	
Tuxedo rental or formal purchase	
Dinner	
Yearbook	
College application fees	

Total Cost _____

Social Studies

Name _____ Date _____ Period _____

Integrating Academics

Catalog Shopping

Many people use catalogs for ordering a variety of goods that are not readily available to them, or to save the time and hassle of shopping. When ordering from a catalog it is important to read the information about returning items that are unsatisfactory. It is also important to calculate the shipping cost when determining the unit price of an item. Fill out the order blank below and calculate the amount of money owed.

| Customer Name and Address | | | Shipping Address | | | | |

Item #	Quantity	Item Description	Color/Style	Size	Unit Price	Total

Delivery Charges

Up to $25	$4.90
$25.01–$75	$6.90
$75.01–$125	$7.90
$125.01–$175	$8.90
$175.01 up	$9.90

Total Price _____

Sales Tax _____

Delivery Charges _____

Total Charge _____

1 Pair of sage chino pants, #994783, Size 36 Reg. $44
1 Black cardigan sweater, # 349726, Size M, $78
2 Pkg ribbed socks, grey/white, #6740408, $12
1 Brown sandal, #50834, Size 9, $38
2 Linen shirts, flax, #90746, Size L, $68
3 White polo short sleeve shirt, #47398, Size L, $24

47

Name _____ Date _____ Period _____

Integrating Academics

Carbohydrates/Fats

Foods containing carbohydrates (starches) and fats can easily be identified by a simple test in your food laboratory.

Collect small samples of the foods you want to test:
    Foods suspected of containing fats
    Foods suspected of containing starch

Supplies:
    A brown paper bag
    Iodine solution in bottle with a dropper

1. Predict in advance the presence of fat or starch or both nutrients found in each food. Write down your predictions.

    _____

    _____

2. **To test for fat:** Cut the paper bag into small squares. Label each square with one of the food subatances you have obtained. Rub some of the food on the paper square. Hold it up to the light. If the paper has become translucent, it indicates the presence of fat or oils.

    _____

    _____

3. **To test for starch:** Slice the food if necessary (example: a potato); place one drop of the iodine solution on the food. If a dark blue-black stain appears on the food, starch is present.

    _____

    _____

Check the results against your predictions.

Science

Integrating Academics

Vitamins

Eating to stay healthy is an easy job when a person eats a variety of foods in each of the food groups. Unfortunately, some of the foods in the fruit and vegetable group are not as well liked as the others. Since nearly all the vitamins in our diet come from this group, many people do not get enough of this nutrient. The Greek word for life is "vita", and the best sources of vitamins are the fruits and vegetables. Look in the table of food values provided by your teacher and compare the vitamin content in the foods listed. The values are listed in a single-serving size. Are you meeting your RDA (recommended daily amount)?

	Vitamin A IU (International units)	**Vitamin C** Mg. (milligram)
1 apple	_____	_____
1 apricot	_____	_____
10 seedless grapes	_____	_____
1 orange	_____	_____
1 peach	_____	_____
1 c. mustard greens	_____	_____
1/2 cantaloupe	_____	_____
1 c. broccoli	_____	_____
1 c spinach	_____	_____
10 french fries	_____	_____

Recommended Daily Allowance of Vitamin A is 5,000 IU

Recommended Daily Allowance of Vitamin C is 60 Mg.

Math

Name _____ Date _____ Period _____

Integrating Academics

Nutrition Scoreboard

I. Many of the foods which are favorites of teenagers are very nutritious. Tacos are served by many restaurants, and school cafeterias and they are a good example of a nutritious snack or meal. The ingredients for one taco are listed below with the food group each represents. The calories contained in these foods may be too high if they are consumed regularly. Use the calorie counter provided by your teacher to calculate the calorie content of the taco.

Taco	Food Group	Calories
1/4 lb. ground beef	meat group	_____
1 small tomato	vegetable	_____
1/4 c. shredded lettuce	vegetable	_____
2 T. shredded cheddar	dairy	_____
1 taco shell	bread	_____
1 T taco seasoning		
TOTAL		_____

II. List the ingredients in one cheeseburger below. Indicate the food groups represented and the number of calories each portion contains.

Hamburger	Food Group	Calories
_____	_____	_____
_____	_____	_____
_____	_____	_____
_____	_____	_____

III. If girls need 2100 calories per day and boys need 2800, what percent of your total calorie needs are represented here? _____

Math

Integrating Academics

Food Pyramids

I. One of the best ways of improving your diet is to become aware of what you are really eating. A good way to do this is to write down everything you eat over a period of time. This list should include all snacks and meals. For the next three school days keep a written record of all your food and liquid intake with the amounts consumed.

Day 1

_____

_____

_____

_____

_____

_____

_____

Day 2

_____

_____

_____

_____

_____

_____

_____

Day 3

_____

_____

_____

_____

_____

_____

_____

II. On a separate piece of paper draw 3 food pyramids similar to the daily food guide found in your textbook. Fill in the blank spaces with the foods that you ate. Now compare your food intake to the recommended choices and servings.

a. How does your diet compare to the nutritional standards?

_____

_____

b. What foods do you need to eliminate?

_____

_____

c. What foods do you need to add to your diet?

_____

_____

Integrating Academics

Water

Approximately 75% of your body is water. It is second only to oxygen in its vital importance to the body. You can live only a few days without water. The body loses an average of 2–2.5 quarts of water a day through waste, perspiration, and vapor from your lungs when you exhale. That same amount is required in foods and beverages to replace the loss.

Draw a bar graph to show the amount of water content in the various foods listed below. Do you eat enough of these foods in addition to 5 to 6 glasses of water a day?

Bread, white	36% water
Milk, whole	87% water
Fruits, fresh	86% water
Beef, lean	60% water
Eggs	74% water
Juice	99% water

Percent of Water

Juice

Milk

Fruits

Eggs

Beef

Bread

0 10 20 30 40 50 60 70 80 90 100

Math

Integrating Academics

Retaining Vitamins

Fragile vitamins are lost when vegetables are cooked. The water-soluble vitamins (C- and B-complex) are the hardest to retain when heat and moisture are applied. Any method of cooking which is short and does not require the addition of liquid will minimize this loss. Stir-frying is a method of cooking which meets this criterion and will also preserve freshness of flavor, crispness of texture, and natural color. Experiment with a one-dish meal which is stir fried by choosing your ingredients from the following categories:

1 meat, 3 vegetables, two seasonings of your choice.

Meats	**Vegetables**	**Seasoning**
1 lb. sliced chicken	1/2 c. sliced mushrooms	2 T. soy sauce
1 lb. sliced pork	1/2 c. chopped celery	4 T. chicken broth
1 lb. sliced beef	1/2 c. sliced onion	4 T. beef broth
	1 c. pea pods	pinch of pepper
	1/2 c. chopped broccoli	
	1/2 sliced green pepper	

1. Heat 2 tablespoons oil in a skillet until hot, add meat and stir for three minutes.

2. Move meat to sides of skillet and place vegetables in the center. Stir for four minutes.

3. Mix meat and vegetables together and add seasonings.

4. Cover, steam for three or four minutes. Serve over hot steamed rice.

What will you name your dish? _____

Science

53

Name _____ Date _____ Period _____

Integrating Academics

Calories

I. Calories power our body. We receive the calories from the food we eat, and we burn the calories for energy. Some activities burn more calories than others. To keep your body weight constant, the calories we eat should equal the calories we burn. Girls need fewer calories as they mature, boys need more. Write down all the food you ate yesterday. Look up the caloric content of each food and calculate the total for the day.

Breakfast:	Calories	Lunch:	Calories
_____	_____	_____	_____
_____	_____	_____	_____
_____	_____	_____	_____
_____	_____	_____	_____

Snacks:	Calories	Dinner:	Calories
_____	_____	_____	_____
_____	_____	_____	_____
_____	_____	_____	_____
_____	_____	_____	_____

Total calories: _____

II. Estimate the amount of calories you burned from the following chart.

Activity	Calories per hour	Activity	Calories per hour
Watching TV	125	Housework	250+
Walking	300	Karate	700
Reading	90	Cooking	125
Eating	100	Soccer	600
Basketball	350+	Office work	150
Running	600+	Sleeping	80

Total calories burned _____

III. Did you balance your food intake with calories burned yesterday? _____

Math

Integrating Academics

Snacking

Snacks are a source of most of our high calorie foods. Since we don't all have the same type of body, some people actually need to eat to gain weight. From the list of snacks found below, identify the ones you would recommend for teens who are trying to gain weight. Beside each food, write down the number of calories found in one serving. Are these the ones you should avoid if you are not trying to gain weight?

Snacks	**Calories**
Angel food cake	_____
Chocolate pudding	_____
Peanuts	_____
Pepperoni pizza	_____
Yogurt	_____
Banana	_____
Raisins	_____
Apple	_____
Devil's food cake	_____
Buttered popcorn	_____
Potato chips	_____
Ice cream	_____
Cola	_____

Snacks recommended to gain weight are:

_____   _____

_____   _____

_____   _____

Math

Integrating Academics

Student Preferences

I. Sometimes it is difficult to come to a consensus when your group is choosing a meal or a food to prepare because of individual food preferences. One way to discover food favorites is to conduct a survey, and prepare a bar graph to illustrate your findings. **Example:** There are 30 students in the class, each is given a ballot with 4 kinds of pies to choose from. The results show that 9 prefer apple, 12 cherry, 4 blueberry, and 5 prefer peach.

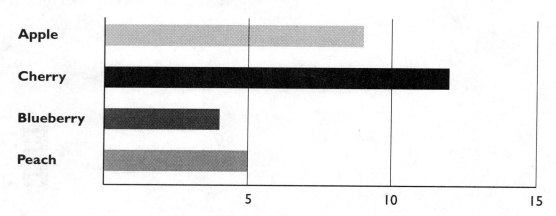

II. Conduct your own class survey. You may choose from cookies, vegetables, international food favorites or teacher's choice. Show the preferences by drawing a bar graph.

Math

Integrating Academics

Planning a Party

Good parties don't just happen. They are planned. Otherwise, everyone has fun but the host or hostess. Let's plan a class party and organize it in such a way that everyone has fun, even the teacher! Look at the list of things to consider below. Is there a job for everyone? Assign a job to each class member. Compare your list with others in the class to decide on final job assignments. More than one person will be required for some of the duties.

Theme Party
(you choose the theme)

Invitations

_____

_____

Menu

_____

_____

_____

_____

_____

Cooks

_____

_____

_____

_____

_____

Decorations

_____

_____

_____

_____

_____

Entertainment

_____

_____

_____

_____

_____

Shopping

_____

_____

Serve

_____

_____

_____

_____

Clean up

_____

_____

_____

_____

_____

Get door prizes

_____

_____

_____

Social Studies

Integrating Academics

Breads Around the World

Americans have come to love the breads from many countries. With so many ethnic groups represented in our country, a common language is often found around the dinner table. Below is a list of breads from around the world. Research the origin of each of the breads listed below. Record any interesting fact you discover about the breads. Select a recipe from those listed, and plan a meal from the country it represents.

1. Tortilla _____

   _____

2. Crêpe _____

   _____

3. Matzo _____

   _____

4. Focaccia _____

   _____

5. Wonton _____

   _____

6. Challah _____

   _____

7. Brioche _____

   _____

8. Panettone _____

   _____

Social Studies

9. Pita _____

_____

10. Crumpet _____

Menu:

Name _____ Date _____ Period _____

Integrating Academics

Grocery Shopping

Organizing your shopping list when you go to the grocery store will make it an easier and quicker job. Picture in your mind a grocery store. All the dairy foods are displayed together, the fruits and vegetables are together, the baked goods are together, etc. If you write your list in the same way, you will not forget anything, and the trip will be shorter. Categorize each of the items listed under the correct heading.

paper towels	chicken	ice cream	cornmeal
detergent	bleach	chili beans	oil
tomato soup	grapes	onions	mushroom soup
bread	potatoes	flour	bathroom cleanser
apples	sugar	milk	foil
buns	spinach	eggs	apple pie
hamburger	lemons	butter	sausage
lettuce	cottage cheese	pizza	frozen corn
oranges	fruit cocktail	pepper	corn on the cob
napkins	cheddar cheese	strawberries	cream
chips	salt	pork chops	

Dairy   **Staples**   **Canned**   **Baked**

_____   _____   _____   _____

_____   _____   _____   _____

_____   _____   _____   _____

_____   _____   _____   _____

_____   _____   _____   _____

_____   _____   _____   _____

60   *Continued on next page*

Language Arts

Meats	Fruits/Vegetables	Frozen	Cleaning/ Paper Products
_____	_____	_____	_____
_____	_____	_____	_____
_____	_____	_____	_____
_____	_____	_____	_____
_____	_____	_____	_____
_____	_____	_____	_____

Integrating Academics

Kitchen Tools

Most students know what the different food preparation tools are used for, however many cannot identify them by their correct names. We will have a kitchen "scavenger hunt" today to help you review the correct names of the equipment you will be working with. Work in pairs to see how quickly you can locate the equipment listed and arrange it on the counter in the order given. Set a time limit. When time is up, someone can check the accuracy of your list.

List #1

grater
wire whisk
pancake turner
bread knife
pastry blender
slotted spoon
rolling pin
mixing bowls
paring knife
mixing spoons
colander
pie pan
ladle
measuring spoons
steamer
tongs
muffin pan
griddle
sauce pan
dry measuring cup
frying pan

List #2

rubber scraper
pastry blender
paring knife
wire whisk
straight-edge spatula
grater
pancake turner
bread knife
rolling pin
strainer
cake pan
steamer
tongs
colander
ladle
sifter
liquid measuring cup
cutting board
biscuit cutter
cookie sheet
muffin pan

Practice spelling all the names correctly!

Language Arts

Integrating Academics

Suspensions and Emulsions

Science

When oil and vinegar or oil and water are agitated (shaken together) they become temporarily suspended. Suspension is when particles are mixed together but stay undissolved in a fluid or solid. After the mixture sits, the liquids separate as the oil particles unite and the water or vinegar particles unite. The addition of a third substance to the mixture can prevent the oil particles from coming together and cause a permanent suspension. The third substance is called an emulsifying agent and the stable mixture is an emulsion. You are familiar with many salad dressings which must be agitated and quickly poured before separation begins. We will make mayonnaise to show how oil and lemon juice mix when a third substance, in this case an egg, is added. The egg becomes an emulsion.

Supplies:
electric blender
1 very fresh egg
1 teaspoon dry mustard
1 teaspoon salt
1 teaspoon sugar
1 cup vegetable oil
3 tablespoons fresh lemon juice

1. Be sure all ingredients and the blender are at room temperature.

2. Place the first four ingredients in the blender container with 1/4 cup of the vegetable oil. Cover and blend on "high" until the mixture is thoroughly combined.

3. Remove the cap in the cover and slowly add 1/2 cup oil while the blender is still running.

4. Add the lemon juice slowly until it is mixed thoroughly.

5. Add the remainder of the oil and blend until thick. You may have to stop and start the blender to scrape down the sides with a rubber spatula.

6. Refrigerate the mayonnaise and use within two weeks.

Many fine restaurants would never use a commercially prepared product, and take great pride in using only freshly made mayonnaise.

Many salad dressing recipes have mayonnaise as an ingredient with additional seasonings to change the flavor. Look in a cookbook and find a recipe which has mayonnaise as the base. Attach a copy to this activity.

Integrating Academics

Safety and Sanitation

It is important to practice good safety and sanitation rules when you are cooking at home or in the home economics laboratory. By following careful work habits many accidents can be avoided and spoilage of food by unsafe sanitation will not occur to cause germs to be spread. Read the chapter in your book on kitchen safety and sanitation. Select one topic from the list below and prepare a short oral presentation to the class demonstrating the safety rule or sanitation practice you have chosen.

Correct way to wash dishes.
How to avoid electric shock.
Storing cleaning products.
Correct way to slice and chop.
How to stir hot food.
Reaching things on a high shelf.
Preventing kitchen fires.
The correct use of pot holders.
Correct way to taste food you are cooking.
How to wash fruits and vegetables
The correct way to wash your hands.

How to prevent pest contamination.
Correct refrigeration practices.
How to extinguish grease fires correctly.
Using small appliances correctly.
How to prevent food poisoning.
How to detect botulism in canned foods.
How to handle spills and breakage.
How to open a can safely.
What to do if you smell gas.
The correct way to dispose of garbage.

Write your report and practice reading it before you give it orally in class.

_____

_____

_____

_____

_____

_____

_____

_____

_____

_____

Language Arts

Integrating Academics

Osmosis

Osmosis occurs when liquids pass through a membrane to equalize concentrations on both sides. When salt is applied to a wet surface, the salt dissolves in the moisture increasing its density and osmosis begins.

Supplies:
    1 apple
    1 eggplant
    1 cucumber
    1 turnip
    Wax paper
    Salt

1. Place two slices of each fruit or vegetable on the wax paper.

2. Sprinkle salt on one slice of each.

3. Observe the slices which have been salted are covered with water and become limp.

4. What do the unsalted slices look like?

_____

_____

_____

When cooking most vegetables, remember to salt after cooking. They will be more tender and require less cooking.

Science

Name _____ Date _____ Period _____

Integrating Academics

Let's Make Macaroni and Cheese

Read about cooking pasta in your foods textbook. Remember that one cup uncooked macaroni will yield two cups cooked. In this recipe we will allow 1/2 cup cooked pasta per serving. This recipe makes four servings. Calculate the amount needed to serve twelve people.

Baked Macaroni

4 Servings   **12 servings**

Boil in salted water:

   4 oz. macaroni (1 cup)   _____ oz. macaroni

Drain macaroni
Preheat oven to 350°
Place layers of macaroni in a buttered baking dish.

Sprinkle the layers with:

   1 cup shredded cheddar cheese   _____ cups cheddar

Beat until blended:

   2 eggs   _____ eggs

   2/3 cup milk   _____ cups milk

   1/4 teaspoon salt   _____ teaspoon salt

   1/8 teaspoon paprika   _____ teaspoon paprika

Pour this mixture over the macaroni. Sprinkle the top with:

Au Gratin

   3 slices dry bread   _____ slices bread

   2 tablespoons butter   _____ tablespoons butter

   1/3 cup cheddar cheese   _____ cup cheddar

Put bread in the blender to make fine bread crumbs. Sprinkle over macaroni mixture, dot with butter, and sprinkle with cheddar cheese. Bake about 40 minutes.

Math

Integrating Academics

Measuring Volume

Volume refers to the amount of space taken up by a product, or, when referring to food, the size of the serving. We are going to perform an experiment today to show how heat and moisture will change the volume of two foods, rice and pasta.

A. Rice

1. Measure 1 C. plain white rice. Look at the volume. Would that amount of rice fill you

    up? _____ Let's see how moisture and heat can affect the volume.

2. Measure 1 cup water in a small saucepan, add a pinch of salt and bring to a boil.

3. Place rice in boiling water, cover, lower heat, simmer for 25 minutes.

How much volume do you now have? _____

You may butter and eat the rice if desired.

B. Pasta

1. Measure 2 oz. (1/2 cup) pasta. Does that look like a serving?

2. Measure 2 cups water in a saucepan, add a pinch of salt. Bring to a boil.

3. Place pasta in boiling water for 8–10 minutes or until done. Drain.

How much volume do you now have? _____

Why did you use twice as much water in the pasta as in the rice? _____

_____

_____

What nutrient caused the rice and pasta to increase in volume? _____

You may butter and eat the pasta if you like.

Name _____ Date _____ Period _____

Integrating Academics

Let's Make Cookies

We need eight dozen cookies for the bake sale on Saturday. Our recipe only makes 36 cookies. Adjust the amounts on the following recipe so that you will have enough for the sale and one extra dozen for you and your friend to sample. (For example: If we needed six dozen, we would multiply by two.)

Chocolate Chip Drop Cookies

Makes 36 cookies
Preheat oven to 375°.

Cream:

1/2 cup butter   _____ cups butter

1/2 cup brown sugar   _____ cups sugar

1/2 cup white sugar   _____ cups sugar

Beat in:

1 egg   _____ eggs

1/2 teaspoon vanilla   _____ teaspoons vanilla

Sift and stir in:

1 cup plus 2 tablespoons flour   _____ cups flour

1/3 teaspoon salt   _____ teaspoon salt

1/2 teaspoon baking soda   _____ teaspoons baking soda

Stir in:

3/4 cup chocolate chips   _____ cups chocolate chips

1/2 cup chopped nuts   _____ cups chopped nuts

Drop the batter from a teaspoon, well apart, on a greased cookie sheet. Bake about 10 minutes.

68

Math

Integrating Academics

Sourdough

I. Sourdough was the usual method of making bread in pioneer days when a cup of "starter" was passed as a gesture of friendship. The mixture was based on flour and water and was fermented (chemically changed) in a way to trap the natural yeast organisms which were plentiful in the air. In our climate-controlled kitchens it is possible to make a "starter", but it is best to rely on a commercial yeast.

Supplies:
  a large mouth jar or crock
  a wooden spoon
  1 package of active dry yeast
  2 cups of water (85 degrees)
  2 cups all-purpose flour

1. Wash the container thoroughly with warm soapy water, rinse and dry, or wash in the dishwasher. Spoilage will occur if any bacteria are left on the container.

2. Combine the yeast, flour, and water.

3. Stir with the wooden spoon (do not use a metal spoon)

4. Let stand uncovered in 80 to 90 degree room temperature for 4 to 7 days or until it begins to bubble.

5. Stir down once a day; if a crust forms, stir it down also.

6. When the starter has a good strong "sour" odor, it is ready to use. If not used at once, cover and refrigerate.

II. Look in a cookbook and select a recipe which uses the sourdough "starter" for the leavening agent. You will find many wheat bread recipes, cornbreads, and cakes. Select a recipe which you can prepare in your kitchen laboratory.

To replenish the starter, take one cup of the original recipe, add one cup flour and one cup lukewarm water. Let stand overnight until it ferments, and use or refrigerate.

Science

Integrating Academics

Leavening Agents

Leavening means to make something rise. A leavening agent is added to a recipe to make that product rise. This is accomplished by the formation of carbon dioxide gas. As the gas is heated the bubbles expand and cause the batter or dough which surrounds them to rise. Baking soda and baking powder are examples of this type of leavening agent. We will prepare a "puff" batter. You will observe an immediate reaction as the carbon dioxide gas is released. The puffs will expand to become very light and will float to the top of the oil. As the puffs brown, the cooked side will flip to the surface and the uncooked side will be underneath as it is heavier.

Supplies:
a small saucepan with tall sides
2 cups vegetable oil for frying
2 teaspoons for dropping batter
1 slotted spoon to remove puffs
paper towels to drain puffs
1 small bowl containing a mixture of sugar and cinnamon

1. Beat 1 egg, add 1/4 c. milk and 1/4 c. vegetable oil.

2. Stir in 1 cup flour, 2 tablespoons sugar, 1 and 1/2 teaspoons baking powder. Mix until flour is moistened.

3. Heat 2 cups vegetable oil in saucepan until small bubbles rise to the top.

4. Use the teaspoons to drop the batter into the hot oil, using one to dip and one to scrape the batter into the oil. Do not make large puffs, they will brown on the outside before the middle is done.

5. When the puffs are brown on both sides, remove from the oil with the slotted spoon and drain on a layer of paper towels.

6. Roll the puffs in the sugar and cinnamon mixture.

Integrating Academics

Lasagna

Lasagna is a favorite food of most teenagers. It is easily prepared and can be made ahead of time from ingredients readily available. We want to plan a lunch with lasagna as the main dish. You and three friends will be eating. The recipe we have serves 16 people. Reduce the recipe to serve four.

Quick Lasagna (serves 16)   **4 servings**

1 32 oz. jar of prepared Italian meat sauce   _____

2 lb. ricotta cheese   _____

1 lb. crumbled mozzarella cheese   _____

2 cups grated Parmesan cheese   _____

1 lb. lasagna noodles   _____

1. Boil the noodles in a large saucepan of water with 2 tablespoons olive oil. Stir to keep the noodles separate. Cook to *al dente* (somewhat firm; not too soft) stage; drain.

2. Preheat oven to 350 degrees.

3. Spread a thin layer of sauce on the bottom of a small baking dish. Layer the noodles and cheeses and the rest of the sauce saving enough Parmesan cheese to sprinkle on the top.

4. Bake about 30 to 40 minutes. Let stand briefly before cutting and serving.

   What other dishes would be appropriate to serve with the lasagna? Write your menu below.

Menu

71

Integrating Academics

Herbs

We use many plants to improve the flavors of foods. Plants used for seasonings are called herbs. They are used both fresh and dried. Because the dried plant is more pungent, the amount of dried herb used in a recipe is less than fresh. Many families grow fresh herbs in pots or a garden. At the end of a growing season it is very easy to dry the herbs in your microwave. These home dried herbs have a fresher flavor than the commercially dried ones.

Supplies:
Small jars with lids or stoppers for storing
Paper towels
Scissors or small paring knife

Method:
Wash the herbs to be dried in cold water.
Dry thoroughly by patting with a paper towel, or use a lettuce spinner.
Use scissors to clip leaves from stems.
Discard stems.
Layer paper towels in the bottom of the microwave.
Arrange herbs in doughnut shape on towels.
Cover with paper towel.
Microwave 1/2 minute; check for dryness.
Rotate towel if necessary.
Repeat the 1/2 minute cycles until the herbs are crisp.
Remove from the microwave; crush with your hands.
Store in airtight container.

Parsley, basil, rosemary, thyme, sage, dill, oregano, mint, chives and tarragon are common herbs to dry. They make gifts appreciated by the gourmet cook.

Use your computer to design attractive labels for your home-prepared kitchen gifts. Attach a copy here:

Label

Science

Integrating Academics

Ripening Fruit

Ethylene is a colorless gas that has a ripening effect on fruit. Apples are known to give off this gas. We will perform an experiment today to see if we can speed up the ripening of bananas in our kitchen laboratory.

Supplies:
  2 medium brown paper bags
  2 green bananas from the same bunch
  1 ripe apple

1. Wash the apple to be sure there was no coating residue from the grocery store if it was polished.

2. Place the apple and one banana in a bag and seal the top tightly.

3. Place the other banana in the second paper bag and seal it tightly.

4. Store both bags in a dark, cool place.

5. Check the bags every couple of days. The length of ripening time will vary depending on how green the bananas were.

6. Which banana ripened first? _____

7. How much longer did the single banana take to ripen? _____

8. Could you use this process to speed up the ripening of other fruits? _____

9. Why do you think fruits are shipped to the grocery stores before they are completely ripe?

_____

_____

_____

_____

10. The next time you are in the grocery store, check the fruit and vegetable department to see how many countries have shipped their products to your town.

73

Science

Integrating Academics

Recycling Food

Have you ever thought that making a new dish out of leftover foods or stale breads or cakes would be classified as recycling? It really is! Whenever waste of food can be prevented by creating a new product, a savings to the environment occurs, and money is saved. Try this recipe for recycling stale bread or biscuits.

Bread Pudding (6 servings)

Preheat oven 350°

Tear bread into cubes, measure 3 1/2 cups
Soak in 3 cups warm milk for 15 minutes
Beat 3 eggs in a bowl
Add 1/2 cup sugar
1 teaspoon vanilla
Grated rind and juice of 1/2 lemon
1/2 cup raisins

Pour egg mixture over bread; stir lightly with a fork until blended. Bake in a casserole set in a pan of hot water for 45 minutes or until firm.

Serve warm with raisin sauce.

Raisin sauce
Mix together:
1 1/2 cups water
1/3 cup raisins
1/4 cup sugar
Boil 15 minutes.
Melt 2 tablespoons butter; stir in 1 teaspoon flour.
Add the hot sauce slowly to the butter/flour mixture
Stir and cook until it boils.
Serve over bread pudding.

Find a recipe for rice pudding to recycle leftover cooked rice!

Social Studies

Integrating Academics

Air As Leavening

Science

A common method of leavening baked goods is found in recipes containing whipped egg whites. Air is trapped in the whipped egg, and as heat is applied to the batter, the air rises. Soon the heat has acted on the protein in the egg whites and flour to stabilize the product, and it does not "fall" on removal from the oven. Prepare an angel food cake to observe this principle.

1. Preheat oven to 350°.

2. **Sift twice:**
    1 1/4 cups sugar

    Add 1 cup cake flour
    1/2 teaspoon salt.

    Sift three more times. (This sifting separates and also adds air.)

3. **Whip** in separate bowl: 1 1/4 cups egg whites (about 10) until foamy.

4. **Add:** 1 teaspoon cream of tartar to eggs, continue beating until stiff, but not dry.

5. **Fold** in 1/2 teaspoon vanilla, 1/2 teaspoon almond extract.

6. **Gently** fold the sugar/flour mixture to the beaten egg whites by tablespoons. Do not beat.

7. **Pour** into a 9-inch ungreased tube pan.

5. **Bake** 45 minutes. Remove from oven and invert to cool. (about 1 1/2 hours)

Cut fresh food angel cakes with pick type divider. (A knife would mash them down.)

This cake has no fat and no cholesterol. All calories come from the carbohydrates in the flour and sugar, and from the protein in the egg whites.

Integrating Academics

Coagulation

Coagulation, the process of changing a liquid into a thickened mass, occurs when animal protein is heated and it becomes firm. The longer it is heated, the firmer it becomes until it toughens. Hard-cooking an egg is a good example of coagulation. The egg white is made up of protein, while the yolk contains the vitamins and minerals. Overcooking the egg makes it tough and causes a discoloration between the yolk and white. The dark color does not affect the flavor, but it is less attractive when preparing a dish such as deviled eggs. We will cook eggs today to a soft-cooked stage, a medium- cooked stage and a hard-cooked stage to watch the process of coagulation as it occurs.

Supplies:
saucepan with lid
timer
3 eggs

1. Place three eggs in a saucepan filled with cold water.
2. Bring the water to a boil, reduce the heat to a simmer, and cover the pan.
3. Set your timer for two minutes.
4. Remove one egg, plunge it into cold water immediately.
5. Set timer for an additional two minutes. At the end of the time, remove a second egg and plunge it into cold water.
6. Continue simmering the third egg for an additional eight minutes.
7. Turn off the burner and remove the last egg from the water and plunge it into cold water.
8. Roll the eggs between your hands to free the tough membrane from the egg and make shelling easier. (Be careful with egg 1!)

1 Soft-Cooked Egg—Record your observations. What degree of firmness did you observe after

two minutes? _____

2 Medium Cooked Egg—What degree of firmness did you observe after this egg was cooked

for four minutes?_____

3 Hard Cooked Egg—Did the protein coagulate entirely in the hard cooked egg? _____

The size of the egg and the degree of coldness may affect the timing. Did you need to cook any

of the eggs longer? _____   Shorter _____?

Science

Integrating Academics

Food Tips

Today, nearly one third of all meals consumed are eaten out. Some of the meals may be from "fast-food" restaurants. These restaurants offer fast service by which you order at a line and bring your food to the table yourself. Other restaurants, in which you are seated at a table and waited on by waiters and waitresses, offer a more leisurely service. The servers who wait on you receive a small salary, but usually a "tip" is the largest part of their pay. If you think the service is good, your tip should be between 15 and 20 percent of the bill. You should always check your bill to be sure it is correct.

1. Add the total bill of each of the restaurant checks below.

2. Determine the correct sales tax for your state.

3. Calculate a fifteen percent tip on each of the checks.

Guest Check

Green salad	4.50
Roast beef	11.50
Coffee	1.00
Lemon pie	3.75
Total	_____
Sales tax	_____
Tip	_____
Total	_____

Guest Check

Tomato-dill soup	4.35
Lemon chicken	9.45
Iced tea	1.00
Carrrot cake	3.55
Total	_____
Sales tax	_____
Tip	_____
Total	_____

Integrating Academics

Microwave Cooking

Microwave cooking is a space age invention which is no longer a "new" technology. We are all familiar with the way this oven has speeded up food preparation. Unfortunately most families rely on the microwave to warm foods and make popcorn rather than to cook dinner. There are many new cookbooks which give instructions for preparing old favorites in new ways. The terminology of the recipes is different, once these terms are learned, following the recipe is easy and the resulting product satisfactory. Find the meaning of the following terms referring to microwave cooking. Write a definition to explain what the word means in a microwave recipe.

Covering: _____

_____

Arranging: _____

_____

Stirring: _____

_____

Turning: _____

_____

Shielding: _____

_____

Rotating: _____

_____

Standing time: _____

Language Arts

Integrating Academics

Evaporation

Indians used the process of evaporation (removing moisture) many years ago to perserve fruits, vegetables, and meats when they placed them in the sun to dry. While this was a lengthy process and not very sanitary, it was effective in preserving the food. We will use an oven today to experiment with drying apples. In order to discourage spoilage and bacteria growth, at least 80% of the water must be removed from the fruit.

Supplies:
    2 firm tart apples
    1 lemon
    a small wooden drying rack
    a scale

1. Core and peel the apples.

2. Slice the apples into rings 1/4 inch thick.

3. Squeeze the lemon juice into a bowl and dip the apples into the juice, covering completely to keep the apples from discoloring. Blot off any extra juice. Weigh the apple rings.

    Weight of apple rings before drying. _____

4. Heat the oven to 150 degrees. Place the apples on the drying rack and place the rack in the center of the oven. Leave the oven door cracked open to let the moisture escape.

5. Turn the apples every 30 minutes until they become rubbery. It may take 5 or 6 hours. If the apples were extremely juicy and drying needs to continue until the next day, turn the oven off overnight and begin the experiment the next morning.

6. Test the dryness of an apple ring by cutting. They are considered dry when they produce no moisture when cut, and feel leathery. Weigh the apples.

    Weight of apple rings after drying _____ Water loss _____%

Integrating Academics

Extracts

The verb *to extract* means to draw out. In our kitchen laboratory we extract flavors when we heat foods in order to blend the flavors to make a pleasing taste. Today, we will make a flavored vinegar for a salad dressing. This product is very expensive if bought in a market already prepared. A small bottle may cost anything from $12 to $20. By using our kitchen, we can duplicate the product at a fraction of the cost. The bottled flavors also make attractive gifts if one ties raffia or ribbon around the top.

Supplies:

A 8 to 12 oz. clear bottle
A cork or cap for the bottle
6 oz. to 10 oz. white wine vinegar (adjust to jar size)
3–4 sprigs basil or other herbs
3 cloves garlic
2 strips red or yellow pepper

1. Sterilize the bottle and cork by boiling 10 minutes in a pan. Be sure the water covers the bottle and cork. Drain, remove bottle with tongs.

2. Place the herbs, garlic, and peppers in the bottle.

3. Boil the vinegar in a saucepan or a glass measuring cup in the microwave.

4. Pour the vinegar into the bottle. Cork the bottle and let stand in a cool, dark place for two weeks.

5. Strain the vinegar into a measuring cup, discard the herbs and spices, return the vinegar to the bottle. Add fresh sprigs of herb. Seal.

6. Use the same method to make other flavors:
   Raspberries and mint.
   Lemon peel and thyme
   Orange peel and basil
   Chives and garlic

This same process can be used for making flavored olive oils.

Science

Integrating Academics

Pretzel Play

A fun activity to organize when entertaining children is to make pretzels. Instead of rolling the pretzels in the usual shape, children can make the letters of their name, hearts, geometric shapes etc. This method can also be used to teach them the alphabet and shapes. At the end of their "lesson" they have a snack that was fun and easy to make.

Supplies:
Liquid measuring cup
Dry measuring cup
Measuring spoon
Coarse salt to sprinkle on top
1 beaten egg
Small brush
Mixing bowl
Baking sheet

Mix the following ingredients:
$1^1/_2$ cups warm water
4 cups all-purpose flour
1 envelope yeast
1 teaspoon salt

1. Have children wash their hands. Give each child a small portion of the dough to roll in whatever shape you have chosen.

2. Brush the shapes with beaten egg and sprinkle with coarse salt.

3. Bake at 425 degrees for 12 minutes.

   As the children eat their pretzels have them identify the shapes.

   Read a story to the children about the country where pretzels came from.

Integrating Academics

Native American Foods

The United States hosts a variety of ethnic cultures, each one of them bringing a taste of their heritage. With so many backgrounds represented, it has been easy to overlook Native American contributions to our food harvest. By the time Columbus arrived in this hemisphere, the inhabitants were thriving on many types of beans and corn. Other foods originating in the Americas include tomatoes, pumpkins, peanuts, cranberries, and maple sugar. A variety of Native American vegetables and fruit are listed below. Plan a tasting party featuring these foods prepared in a Native American dish. Research cookbooks in the library for recipes.

Recipe

Posole Corn

_____

_____

_____

Chayote Squash

_____

_____

_____

Anasazi Beans

_____

_____

_____

Pumpkin

_____

_____

_____

Blueberries

_____

_____

_____

Social Studies

Integrating Academics

Ethnic Food Fair

I. Does everyone in your class eat the same food? Probably not. We learn about food habits in families, and classes are usually made up of people from many different cultures with many different food tastes. Survey your class. How many countries are represented? The foods listed below were favorites of one class of students. Can you identify the country?

	Country		**Country**
Sushi	_____	Hassenpfeffer	_____
Quiche	_____	Frittata	_____
Kiwi	_____	Croissant	_____
Paella	_____	A La Mode	_____
Shish Kebabs	_____	Gumbo	_____
Kibbie	_____	Kipper	_____
Guacamole	_____	Fettucine	_____

Social Studies

II. Plan a food fair in your class by having each student bring a family recipe to class. Select one for each group to prepare. Research some background information on each country represented so that you can decorate the table with items representative of that country. Class members may bring a family member to tell about their country of origin and share remembered traditions. Foreign language students may want to print the recipe in the language of the country represented. If your school has foreign exchange students, they can be invited to participate and share the food traditions of their countries.

Name _____ Date _____ Period _____

Integrating Academics

Table Setting

Read the information in your textbook on table setting. Three menus are listed below, draw a correct table setting for each menu showing the correct placement of flatware, glass, napkin. and plates for one person.

Menu: Tossed Salad
Spaghetti with meat sauce
Garlic bread
Iced tea
Pistachio ice cream

Menu: Hamburger on a bun
Potato Salad
Broccoli Ccasserole
Lemonade
Cheese cake

Menu: Orange and spinach salad
Beef tenderloin
Puff potatoes
Asparagus
Coffee
Chocolate raspberry torte

Social Studies

Name _____ Date _____ Period _____

Integrating Academics

Etiquette Review

Answer the questions below concerning the accepted customs of behavior at the table. Write your answer as a complete sentence.

1. Why should your hands be washed before eating?

_____

_____

2. Where is the napkin placed while you are eating?

_____

_____

3. How do you signal the waiter or waitress that you have finished a meal?

_____

_____

4. Explain the correct way to eat soup.

_____

_____

5. Which foods are considered "finger foods?"

_____

_____

6. At which time is it considered proper to begin eating?

_____

_____

85   *Continued on next page*

Language Arts

7. How would you know which flatware to use for the first course?

   _____

   _____

8. Explain the correct way to eat a roll.

   _____

   _____

9. Where is the knife placed after you have used it?

   _____

   _____

10. How should you proceed to eat food which is too hot?

   _____

   _____

Integrating Academics

Clothing Classics

Some clothing styles are called **classic** because they never seem to go out of style. Your grandparents wore them, then your parents, and now you find them in your closet. Some examples of classic styles are the blazer, polo-style shirts, pullover sweaters and pleated skirts. Most wardrobes contain a few classic styles. These styles are usually attractive on all figure types. Because of their timelessness, they are a good buy for the consumer.

Look in a current fashion magazine. Find pictures of the new clothing styles for the coming season which are variations of classic styles. Cut out the pictures, attach them to a sheet of paper, and describe the changes made, if any. Say if you think the style will look good on all figure types. **Example:** a very short pleated skirt may be attractive on an average figure, but not on a heavy person.

Social Studies

Integrating Academics

Fads

Every year new fashions become popular reflecting the current trends in our society. Many of these fashions are only popular for a short period of time. These fashion trends, which are quite short-lived, become a very expensive investment. They become outdated before they have been worn very many times, even though some of these "fads" may become popular again after a few years. Your parents could probably tell you about some of the fashion cycles they have observed.

I. How many "fads" have you observed? Can you list five?

1. _____

2. _____

3. _____

4. _____

5. _____

II. Look up the description of the following fashions and indicate the year they became popular.

1. Saddle shoes and bobby sox _____

2. Poodle skirts _____

3. Bell bottoms _____

4. Miniskirts _____

5. Leisure suits _____

6. Bustles _____

Language Arts

Integrating Academics

A Spending Plan

Imagine that you have $300 to spend on clothes for the new school year. What would you buy? How would you go about deciding what you need?

Step 1. Look in your closet. Are there clothes you have not worn for two years? If so, you should probably give them away or decide if they can be recycled into something wearable.

Step 2. List all the items that are wearable and that you really like. It is a good idea to list tops and bottoms separately with the idea of mixing and matching to gain versatility.

Step 3. Decide if you can purchase a top or a bottom to go with the things already in your closet thus possibly lengthening their wear.

Step 4. Examine your shoes for wear. Do you need to discard any? Match the shoes to your existing clothing.

Step 5. Look at all your accessories. Can they be used with more than one item of clothing? Do you need to add to your collection?

Step 6. Make a list of all the items you need, together with the approximate cost and length of time they can be worn.

Wardrobe Inventory:	Clothing Needs	Cost
_____	_____	_____
_____	_____	_____
_____	_____	_____
_____	_____	_____
_____	_____	_____
_____	_____	_____
_____	_____	_____
_____	_____	_____

Were you able to get the things you need for the year with your $300?_____

Integrating Academics

Sewing

There are many reasons why people choose to sew at home. When making a decision as to whether to sew or to buy a garment there are a number of things to be considered. Each of us has resources to help us do our tasks. Time and energy are two of our most precious resources. Money is also a resource. Each of these has limits. Good management occurs when we use our resources wisely. Consider the problem of obtaining a shirt. Answer the questions below about the use of your resources in order to help you make the decision to make a shirt or to purchase one.

1. How much time will it take to shop for a ready-made shirt? _____

2. How much time will it take to find a pattern and a fabric? _____

3. How long will it take to construct the shirt at home? _____

4. Will you need assistance with shopping or sewing? _____

5. Do you have sewing equipment available? _____

6. Is the purchased shirt worth the cost ($29.00)? _____

7. If the fabric, pattern, and notions cost $13.00, will making the shirt be really saving? _____

8. Is it important to have made something you can be proud of? _____

9. Would you rather have a shirt like everyone else's? _____

10. Would sewing help you prepare for a career later in the fashion field? Why or why not?

    _____

    _____

11. What is your decision? _____

    _____

    _____

Language Arts

Integrating Academics

Determining Clothing Cost

There is a great deal of conflict between parents and teens over clothing costs. A good way for both sides to see the whole situation is to determine the cost per wearing of those clothing items which may be in question.

Fill in the chart below to the best of your ability. Some of your figures will be estimates.

	Jeans	**Athletic shoes**
Garment Cost	_____	_____
Number of times you wore in a month.	_____	_____
Number of months you wore the item.	_____	_____
Number of years you will wear the item.	_____	_____

Calculate the cost per wearing by dividing the amount you paid by the total number of wearings. (**Example:** if you buy dress shoes for $60, you wear them four times a month for twelve months for two years: $60 divided by $4 \times 12 \times 2 = 96$ wearings = .62 per wearing)

Show your calculation for the jeans and athletic shoes below.

Jeans   **Shoes**

Cost per wearing for jeans _____; cost per wearing for shoes _____.

Does that seem a reasonable amount to pay per wearing? _____

Math

Name _____ Date _____ Period _____

Integrating Academics

Designer Jeans:
What's the Difference?

Probably the most popular type of clothing worn by teens today is the blue jean. Americans buy more than 400 million pairs a year. That figure translates into many millions of dollars. The retail consumer generally pays twice the wholesale price. If a store pays $10, it might mark the retail price up to $20. This markup goes to pay for the cost of doing business: salaries, heating and cooling, advertising, shoplifting, lighting, and security. Some stores have more expenses than others because of their location and the type of services they offer. The price that you pay for jeans may also contain another markup if they have a designer label. This is because of the additional advertising cost and endorsement fee for celebrities.

I. Below is a list of jean labels. Research the average cost of each label by doing comparison shopping at clothing stores or asking friends who have already purchased a particular label.

	Cost		**Cost**
Lee	_____	Guess	_____
Wrangler	_____	Bill Blass	_____
Chic	_____	Bugle Boy	_____
Calvin Klein	_____	Levi's	_____
Gap	_____	Banana Republic	_____

II. Write a paragraph explaining the psychological appeal of designer labels.

_____

_____

_____

_____

_____

_____

_____

Name _____ Date _____ Period _____

Integrating Academics

Threading the Machine

Watch a demonstration on threading your sewing machine. Could you explain to another person the process you have just observed? Look in your textbook at the chapter on the machine. Review the parts of the machine and the function of each part. Write step-by-step directions on how to thread the machine. (The parts are listed below.) After you have written your directions, have a classmate try to thread the machine by following your guide.

Machine Parts

bobbin	spool pins	bobbin winder	take-up lever
needle	thread guides	hand wheel	bobbin case
slide plate	presser foot	tension	spool of thread

_____

_____

_____

_____

_____

_____

_____

_____

_____

_____

_____

1. Were your directions clear? _____

2. Did you omit any steps? _____

3. Is the machine ready to sew? _____

4. Make any corrections necessary in your instructions.

93

Language Arts

Name _____ Date _____ Period _____

Integrating Academics

Special Occasion Clothing

You may have heard the saying "clothes make the man." In many instances this is true when you consider how we use clothing to identify a person's position at a particular time or place. Below are listed some of these situations. Write a complete sentence explaining how we identify that persons by their clothing.

1. A policeman directing traffic _____

_____

_____

2. A ballerina ____ _____

_____

_____

3. A naval officer _____

_____

_____

4. A bride _____

_____

_____

5. A nurse _____

_____

_____

6. A priest saying Mass _____

_____

_____

94

Continued on next page

Language Arts

7. A student in the band _____

_____

_____

8. A cheerleader _____

_____

_____

9. A worker at McDonald's _____

_____

_____

10. A football player _____

_____

_____

11. An airline pilot _____

_____

_____

12. A fireman _____

_____

_____

Could you be identified by your clothing? _____ Explain. _____

_____

_____

_____

_____

Integrating Academics

Recycling

Many clothing items may not be wearable, but often the fabric and the fiber are still in good shape. These worn garments are excellent for patchwork craft projects. Collect a variety of clothing so that you will have different patterns and colors to make your designs more interesting. The garment should be washed. Buttons, zippers and other trim items should then be removed. Select a project to fit into your time allotment.

I. Project—Patchwork Pillow

1. Decide on the finished size of your pillow.

2. Make a template of the size squares you wish to piece together. Use this as a pattern for cutting your squares so they will all be the same size.

3. Cut out all the squares. Place them on a flat surface to make your color or pattern design. Press the squares.

4. Sew together one strip of squares at a time. When the strips are completed, match the corner, pin and stitch.

5. Using a solid color back, stitch the front and back together (remember, right sides together). Leave a four-inch opening to turn to the right size.

6. Before turning, clip the corners to get a nice seam. Turn, press both sides, and stuff with cotton. Stitch together the four-inch opening using a basting stitch.

II. Project—Lap Robe

Follow the instructions above for a pillow except for stuffing. The size of the lap robe should be at least four by five feet. This is a good project for your class to do as a service to an area nursing home.

Integrating Academics

Clothing Construction

Although clothing styles have changed a great deal through the centuries, the basic methods of construction have remained the same. They all fall into three categories: the fitted garment which has been seamed together, the draped or wrapped garment, and a combination of the two. From the list of garment names below, identify the country each one came from, or the time it was worn, and tell if it is fitted, draped, or a combination of fitted and draped.

Clothing Styles	Country or Time	Fitted, Draped, or Combination
1. Bloomers		
2. Churidar and kurta pants		
3. Parka		
4. Princess-line dress		
5. Poncho		
6. Sari		
7. Kimono		
8. Sarong		
9. Toga		
10. Mumu		
11. Chilton		
12. Shirtwaist dress		

Social Studies

Integrating Academics

Floor Covering

One of the most dramatic ways of changing the decor of a room is to change the floor covering. Sales are constantly advertised. Floor coverings are priced by the square yard, and room sizes are measured by square feet so a little math is required. Remember that to get the square footage of a room, the width is multiplied by the length. **Example:** if a room is 12×18, the square feet are 216. To calculate the number of square yards 216 is divided by 9. (There are 3 feet in one yard.)

Calculate the number of square yards in the following rooms. Then find the cost of re-covering the floor at the price given per square yard.

Room # 1 10×16
Covering is $12.99 per square yard

Cost _____

Room # 2 12×24
Covering is $16.99 per square yard.

Cost _____

Room # 3 9×13
Covering is $24.99 per square yard

Cost _____

Math

Integrating Academics

Wallpapering

Many do-it-yourself projects around the house are fun, easy, and can save money for the person brave enough to learn the process. One method of changing a room decor is to cover the walls with paper, cloth, or vinyl wallcoverings. Wallpapers are sold in rolls. A single roll will cover 30 square feet.

To estimate the number of rolls needed:

1. Measure the distance around the room (including door openings).

2. Measure the height of the ceiling.

3. Multiply the ceiling height by the distance around the room (round off to the nearest foot) and divide by 30. From this number, subtract 1/2 roll for each regular size window and door.

The result (rounded to the next whole number) is the number of single rolls you need to cover the entire room.

Example: A room is 10 feet wide and 12 feet long with a ceiling height of 8 feet.

$2 \times 10 = 20$
$2 \times 12 = \underline{24}$
$\qquad 44 \times 8 = 352 \div 30 = \qquad 11.73$ rolls
There is one window and one door $- \quad \underline{1.00}$
$\qquad\qquad\qquad\qquad\qquad\qquad 10.73$ rolls rounded to 11 rolls.

Calculate the number of rolls of wallpaper needed to paper a room with these proportions.

width—14 feet
length—18 feet
height—8 feet
There are 2 windows and 1 door.

Number of rolls needed _____

Name _____ Date _____ Period _____

Integrating Academics

Location

What kind of neighborhood would you like to live in when you have a home of your own? What are the factors which make one neighborhood more desirable than others? If you look at comparable houses in different locations you will find large price differences due mainly to the location of the property. Some of the factors that determine housing cost are listed below. Prioritize them in the order of their importance to you. (List the most important first and the rest in descending order of importance.)

Factors	**Important to You**
1. Close to work	1. _____
2. Safe and secure	2. _____
3. Little traffic	3. _____
4. Racially mixed	4. _____
5. Trees	5. _____
6. Close to shopping	6. _____
7. Close to public transportation	7. _____
8. Large yard	8. _____
9. No pollution nearby	9. _____
10. Sidewalks	10. _____
11. Attractive homes near	11. _____
12. Good schools	12. _____

List any additional factors that are important to you.

_____

_____

_____

Social Studies

Integrating Academics

Floor Plans

A floor plan is a design of your room and the furniture and equipment drawn to scale within the room. Plans for organizing a room will depend upon what the space is going to be used for. These plans are usually drawn on graph paper. This paper allows you to assign a certain number of squares to represent a foot so that everything in the room will be in the correct proportion or scale. (**Example:** 2 squares = 1 foot) Draw a floor plan on a piece of graph paper. Be sure to show the placement of the doors and windows. The room plan may be a living room, dining room, den, or bedroom.

Considerations:

a. Activities the room will be used for (study, sleep, play, eat, entertain, music, exercise).

b. Traffic pattern (how you will move around)?

c. Furniture required, allowing the correct number of squares per foot for each piece.

d. Doors and closets should have room to open.

e. Storage may be included.

f. Count the squares between the pieces of furniture to be sure there is room to move around.

Indicate the length and width of the room, and calculate the square feet. (Width × length = X square feet)

Math

Sample Room

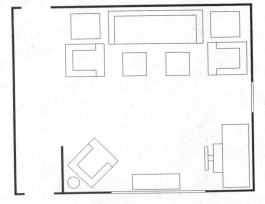

Name _____ Date _____ Period _____

Integrating Academics

Renting Apartments

Diane Thomas is a single mother of three children. Jed is eight, and Salina and Jeffrey are six. She is searching for an apartment in the city close to her job as a computer analyst for an insurance company. She does not have a car. Her income is $2400 a month. Her rent should not exceed ¼ of her monthly income. Read the ads for apartments below and select the one which would best suit her family's needs.

2 BR walk-up, close to bus line. $500 a month. Security, all utilities paid.	3 BR, 2 BA, Laundry, playground, parking, Deposit, $995 mo.	2 BR, den, elec. kit, water, furnished, busline, walk to shopping center, $595.

1. Which apartment would you select?_____

2. What factors did you consider the most important to consider in making your decision?

_____

_____

_____

3. What are some other items of information that Ms. Thomas needs to obtain before making a final choice?

_____

_____

_____

4. Did your choice provide for the family's needs for privacy, protection, work and play space?

Explain._____

_____

_____

_____

Continued on next page

Social Studies

5. What alternative to apartment living could Ms. Thomas consider?

_____

_____

_____

_____

_____

Name _____ Date _____ Period _____

Integrating Academics

Buying a House

The American dream almost always includes a home of one's own. Because very few people have the money to pay cash for a house, a mortgage is usually required. There are certain guidelines used by lending institutions which have been designed to keep families from getting into financial difficulties later on. These guidelines not only consider a family income but whether a couple has dependants. Single people can usually afford to pay proportionately more of their income toward the purchase of a home than a family with children.

Single persons or married couples with no children are allowed up to **33%** of their gross monthly income as the limit for a house payment. This amount should include the principal, interest, property taxes, and homeowners' insurance.

A couple with children should not exceed **28%** of their gross monthly income for the house payment.

Calculate the payments which the families below could make using these guidelines.

1. The Ruiz family consists of a mother with three children. Her income from a job as a physician is $94,000 a year.

    Payment _____

2. Joe and Linda Smith have combined incomes of $42,000. Their children are grown and do not live at home.

    Payment _____

3. Brenda and Mike have four children. She does not work, and Mike makes $38,000 a year as a teacher.

    Payment _____

Integrating Academics

On Your Own

It is an exciting time to think of getting that first place of your own. It is also a shocking experience to discover just how much your parents have been providing for you. To cushion the shock, it would be a valuable exercise to research some of the hidden expenses that you will incur.

It will be necessary to pay a deposit on some of the "necessities." For persons who have no established credit rating, the deposit will provide a cash back up to the company which provides **service credit** to you.

1. How much will the charge be to get a telephone in your name? _____

2. How much will the utility company charge to have the lights, gas, and water connected in

   your name? _____

3. How many months' rent will you have to pay before you can move into the apartment?

   _____

4. Does the apartment require a security deposit? If so, how much? _____

5. What is the connection charge to have cable TV? _____

6. How much will it cost each time you use the washer and dryer to do your laundry? _____

7. List all the cleaning products you will need and their cost.

   _____

   _____

   _____

   _____

8. Do you have to pay extra for pets? _____

9. Renter's insurance is required if your want your possessions covered in case of fire. How

   much would that cost? _____

105

Math

Integrating Academics

Saving Electricity

I. If your electricity has ever "blacked out" during a storm, you know how much we depend on this source of energy in our homes. Nearly all of our appliances are powered by electricity. The cost in dollars is significant, and the cost to our environment in producing the power is enormous. Can you inventory every appliance in your home that depends on electricity? List them under the correct category.

Personal Care	**Lighting**	**Kitchen**	**Security**
_____	_____	_____	_____
_____	_____	_____	_____
_____	_____	_____	_____
_____	_____	_____	_____
_____	_____	_____	_____

Cleaning	**Heating & Cooling**	**Entertainment**	**Lawn care**
_____	_____	_____	_____
_____	_____	_____	_____
_____	_____	_____	_____
_____	_____	_____	_____

II. The utility company providing your electricity has produced pamphlets explaining how to conserve electrical power. Consult this source of information and determine at least one energy-saving tip for each appliance on your list. Make a poster depicting these energy-saving tips to display in your school on "Earth Day."

Language Arts

Integrating Academics

Marriage Success

Sociologists who have studied the subject of marriage have suggested that there may be predictors of success or failure in marriages. Do you think a couple should end a relationship if statistically they are not a good match? Research the predictors listed below, and summarize your findings.

Age at marriage: _____

_____

_____

Similarity of background: _____

_____

_____

Parents' marriage successful: _____

_____

_____

Religious beliefs: _____

_____

_____

Education: _____

_____

_____

Length of courtship and engagement: _____

_____

_____

Social Studies

Integrating Academics

Help Wanted

I. At certain times of the year the "Help Wanted" signs begin to appear. The turnover in the workforce due to school opening or closing generates many of these requests for help. If you were the manager of a place of business that hired a lot of teenage employees, what qualifications would you be looking for? List below the qualifications you would require.

1. _____

    _____

2. _____

    _____

3. _____

    _____

4. _____

    _____

II. Compose an advertisement to run in the newspaper that would appeal to teenagers looking for work, and which would communicate the type of employee you were looking for.

_____

_____

_____

_____

_____

_____

_____

Language Arts

Integrating Academics

Thank You

Language Arts

It is important in maintaining family relationships to remember to show appreciation for gifts, favors, or just everyday kindness. A person who is thanked for doing things will feel better about themselves and will have a positive attitude toward repeating that behavior. It is also a good habit to develop in reinforcing positive personality traits. We "like" people who show us that we are appreciated. One way to say thank-you is by writing a note or a letter.

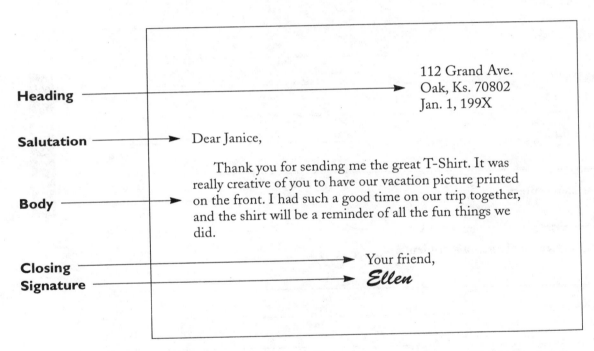

Heading

112 Grand Ave.
Oak, Ks. 70802
Jan. 1, 199X

Salutation

Dear Janice,

Body

Thank you for sending me the great T-Shirt. It was really creative of you to have our vacation picture printed on the front. I had such a good time on our trip together, and the shirt will be a reminder of all the fun things we did.

Closing
Signature

Your friend,
Ellen

A friendly letter is informal, but there is a correct format to use. Review the sample letter below.

On a separate sheet of paper compose a "thank-you" note to someone who has shown a kindness to you.

Example: It could be a note to your grandmother for the birthday check or to a teacher for helping you with a problem.

Remember to use correct spelling, punctuation, and capitalization.

Integrating Academics

Volunteering

A great way to prepare for a first job is to volunteer your services at a community service agency. You can develop work skills which will teach you about such things as meeting deadlines, and being on time. Volunteer jobs help you learn about the importance of being responsible, and they provide great references when you get ready to apply for that first paying job. What places in your neighborhood are looking for volunteers? Look up a telephone number for the following places in your area and inquire about their volunteer programs. Record the information you receive.

1. **Hospital:** _____

_____

2. **Nursing home:** _____

_____

3. **Day care center:** _____

_____

4. **Senior citizen center:** _____

_____

5. **Tutoring service for elementary students:** _____

_____

6. **Religious institution:** _____

_____

7. **Your own school:** _____

_____

8. **Services for the homebound or the elderly:** _____

_____

Social Studies

Name _____ Date _____ Period _____

Integrating Academics

Career Choices

Fast paced changes in technology are creating a job market in which few individuals follow a life-long career path. Predictions for the near future are that young people entering the world of work today can expect as many as four careers in their lifetime. Perhaps you will end up working in a job that has not yet been created! Learning all you can now, will make it easier to make a decision on what career paths are best suited to you.

Using the DOT or OOH found in the library, find out the following information about three jobs you are most interested in at the present.

	Job # 1 _____	Job # 2 _____	Job # 3 _____
Duties:			
Hours:			
Salary range:			
Qualifications:			
Education:			
Promotions:			
Work environment:			

Social Studies

Integrating Academics

Your Résumé

The first step in writing your résumé is to gather all the information about your accomplishments. After the facts have been written down, it is easy to organize the information in an attractive layout and rewrite it in the most effective language. Prepare a résumé using the following guidelines.

Name: Include your first, middle, and last names.

Address: This information tells the prospective employer where you can be contacted by mail.

Phone Number: Give the number for a phone or answering machine that will always be answered during normal business hours.

Objective: This information tells where you are heading. It should be written in a single, concise sentence describing your employment goals.

Work Experience: List all of your jobs in reverse chronological order. Be accurate in listing your job, your responsibilities and any special accomplishments. Show all part-time jobs, summer employment, and regular volunteer work. Employees know that at your age you do not have years of experience, but all work is important. Show the dates you were employed and the duties you performed.

Education: If you are still in school, state that fact. If you are graduating, give the expected date. Include any major area of concentration in high school, and mention any special skills you have.

Honors or Activities: If you received any special honors or held any office, they should be included to indicate leadership qualities.

Personal Information: List your hobbies, social skills, or extracurricular activities.

References: You do not have to list your references on the résumé, but you should write that they are available upon request. Keep your own list of references handy, and be sure to get permission to use a person as a reference before listing his or her name.

Language Arts

Integrating Academics

Careers in Housing

The home building industry accounts for a large number of workers each year in a variety of jobs. Some of the categories are listed below. Look in the **DOT** or **OOH** in the library and select a job or career in this industry that you want to know more about. Write a one-page article telling about what you discovered.

Real estate sales	Painters
Designing houses	Roofer
Interior design	Excavation
Carpenter	Paving
Electrician	Concrete worker
Plumber	Finisher
Mason	Cabinet Maker
Paperhangers	Carpet layer
Plasterers	Flooring
Landscaping	Kitchen planner
Building inspector	Appraiser
Mortgage loan originator	Closing attorney

Language Arts

Integrating Academics

Real Estate Terminology

Refer to the list of terms below to fill in the blanks of this home-buying case study. If you do not know the meaning of the words, look them up in your textbook or a reference book in the library.

Mortgage	Title	Insurance	Sales comission
Closing cost	Real estate agent	Guarantee	Taxes
Termite	Taxes	Interest	
Credit	Appraiser	Deed	
Loan application	Down payment	Principal	

Chuck and Cindy decided that the safest way to buy their first house was to find a good

_____. Once they started looking, they did not take long to find the perfect

house. They decided to limit their price range so the payment would not exceed 25% of their

income. They went to a lending institution to fill out a _____. They found

they could _____ a loan rate at closing if they paid a fee. Soon they discoved

other costs. The house 's value would have to be determined by an _____.

Their _____ would have to be checked for financial stability. They decided to

pay 20% _____ to lower the amount of money they needed to borrow. The

_____ they paid their real estate agent was a good investment. She arranged

for a _____ inspection and builiding inspection. She also contacted the real

estate attorney to handle the _____ search and to see that the

_____ was recorded at the courthouse. They discovered that some of the

_____ would have to be prorated and that homeowners'

_____ was required by the lending institution. Their house payment would

include _____, _____, _____ and insur-

ance. When the day arrived for closing they had all their papers in order and checks written to

pay the _____. They now had a home and a _____ which

they would pay on for 30 years.

Language Arts

Answers

Integrating Academics

Making Money

Name _____ Date _____ Period _____

Many classrooms devise ways to make money for class projects or trips when funds are unavailable. Two examples are given below. Calculate the amount of money each class made. Show all your work so you can check your answer.

1. **Mrs. Smith's Class:** The class decided to buy 12 boxes of candy bars for $3.00 a box. Each box contained 12 bars and each candy bar was sold for $.75. How much profit did the class make?

> 1 box sold $9.00 (12 x .75 = 9)
> 1 box cost   −3.00
> $6.00 profit on each box
>
> 12 boxes x $6.00 = $72.00 profit
>
>   Profit: __$72.00__

2. **Mr. Allen's Class:** The class bought six rolls of slice-and-bake cookies for $1.89 each. Each roll made 24 cookies after they were baked. They were able to sell all the cookies for $.25 each. How much money did they make?

> 1 roll sold $6.00 (12 x .75 = 9)
> 1 roll cost   −1.89
> $4.11 profit on each roll
>
> 6 rolls x $4.11 = $24.66 profit
>
>   Profit: __$24.66__

3. If the class needed to make $100.00 profit, how much of either product would they have to sell?

> Candy: $100 ÷ $6 profit on each box = 16.67 or 17 boxes
>
>   Candy: __17 boxes__
>
> Cookies: $100 ÷ $4.11 profit on each box = 24.33 rolls or 25
>
>   Cookies: __25 rolls__

Math

37

Name _____ Date _____ Period _____

Integrating Academics

Class Trip

I. The seventh-grade class at Butler Middle School is planning to take a trip to the amusement park at the end of the year. There are 120 class members so they will have to rent four school busses at $50.00 each. The tickets will be $28.00 each for the students and 12 adult chaperones. How much will the class have to raise for everyone to go?

> 120 + 12 = 132 people
>
> 132 x $28 = $3,696.00 Tickets
> 4 x $50 = $200.00 Bus
> $3,896.00 Total

Math

II. What will the cost be for each person who decides to pay his or her own way (including $10.00 apiece for food)?

> $3,896 ÷ 132 = $29.51
>   +10.00 Food
> $39.51
>
> Bus cost per person: 200 ÷ 132 = $ 1.51
> Ticket   28.00
> Food   10.00
> $39.51

Name _____ Date _____ Period _____

Integrating Academics

Unit Pricing

To determine the best price of items being purchased, it is necessary to calculate the price per ounce, per pound, or by number of items per package. Once the unit price has been calculated, a decision can be made determining the best value. Most grocery items have the unit price listed on the store shelf under the item. If this is not the case, the unit price can easily be calculated. Divide the total price by the number of ounces etc.

Example: 16 oz. of spaghetti cost 69 cents, $^{69}/_{16}$ = 4.31 per ounce.

Calculate the unit price of the following items to determine the best buy:

1. a. 22 oz. cereal for $3.49 _____.16_____

   b. 14 oz cereal for $1.88 _____.13_____

   Best buy _____14 oz._____

2. a. 1 qt. of milk for $ 1.04 _____1.04_____

   b. 1 gallon of milk for $2.19 _____.55_____

   Best buy _____1 gal._____

3. a. 1 lb. potatoes for $ .59 _____.59_____

   b. 5 lb. potatoes for $2.29 _____.46_____

   Best buy _____5 lb._____

4. a. 13 oz. can of coffee for $2.79 _____.21_____

   b. 39 oz. can of coffee for $9.50 _____.24_____

   Best buy _____13 oz._____

Math

44

Name _____ Date _____ Period _____

Integrating Academics

Sales For Sale

Everyone loves a sale! Many shoppers search advertising supplements daily to determine the best buys for items on their shopping list. It may take some math skills to be able to figure out the exact discount for each purchase. Look at the methods of advertising discounts listed below. Calculate the percentage "off" for each unit purchased.

1. **Buy One Get One Free**   _____ 50 %
   If you spend $10 on one shirt, and get the second one free, how much did each shirt actually cost?   _____ $5.00

   $10.00 ÷ 2 = $5.00

   $5.00 ÷ $10.00 = 50%

2. **Buy One Regular Price, Second Item Half Off**   _____ 75 %
   If you spend $40 on a pair of jeans, and get the second pair for half off, how much did you actually pay for each pair?   _____ $30.00

   $40.00 + $20.00 = $60.00
   $60.00 ÷ 2 = $30.00

   $30.00 ÷ $40.00 = 75%

3. **Buy Three, Get Fourth Item Free**   _____ 75 %
   If you buy three candy bars for $.60 each and receive a fourth candy bar free, how much did each candy bar cost?   _____ $0.45

   3 x $0.60 = $1.80
   $1.80 ÷ 4 = $0.45

   $0.45 ÷ $0.60 = 75%

4. **Buy Two, Get Third Item Free**   _____ 66.67 %
   If you pay $3.00 each for two pairs of socks and get a third pair free, how much did each pair of socks cost?   _____ $2.00

   2 x $3.00 = $6.00
   $6.00 ÷ 3 = $2.00

   $2.00 ÷ $3.00 = 66.67%

Math

   45

Integrating Academics

Catalog Shopping

Many people use catalogs for ordering a variety of goods that are not readily available to them, or to save the time and hassle of shopping. When ordering from a catalog it is important to read the information about returning items that are unsatisfactory. It is also important to calculate the shipping cost when determining the unit price of an item. Fill out the order blank below and calculate the amount of money owed.

Math

Customer Name and Address			Shipping Address			

Item #	Quantity	Item Description	Color/Style	Size	Unit Price	Total
994783	1	Chino pants	Sage	36	44.00	44.00
349726	1	Cardigan sweater	Black	M	78.00	78.00
6740408	2	Ribbed socks	Grey/White		12.00	24.00
50834	1	Sandal	Brown	9	38.00	38.00
90746	2	Shirts	Flax	L	68.00	136.00
47398	3	Polo shirts	White	L	24.00	72.00

Delivery Charges

Up to $25	$4.90
$25.01–$75	$6.90
$75.01–$125	$7.90
$125.01–$175	$8.90
$175.01 up	$9.90

Total Price _____ 392.00
(.06 State Tax x $368.00)

Sales Tax _____ 23.52

Delivery Charges _____ 9.90

Total Charge _____ $425.42

1 Pair of sage chino pants, #994783, Size 36 Reg. $44
1 Black cardigan sweater, # 349726, Size M, $78
2 Pkg ribbed socks, grey/white, #6740408, $12
1 Brown sandal, #50834, Size 9, $38
2 Linen shirts, flax, #90746, Size L, $68
3 White polo short sleeve shirt, #47398, Size L, $24

47

Name _____ Date _____ Period _____

Integrating Academics

Let's Make Macaroni and Cheese

Read about cooking pasta in your foods textbook. Remember that one cup uncooked macaroni will yield two cups cooked. In this recipe we will allow 1/2 cup cooked pasta per serving. This recipe makes four servings. Calculate the amount needed to serve twelve people.

Baked Macaroni

4 Servings

12 servings

Boil in salted water:

Each amount needs to be multiplied by 3.

  4 oz. macaroni (1 cup)

    __12__ oz. macaroni

Drain macaroni
Preheat oven to 350°
Place layers of macaroni in a buttered baking dish.

Math

Sprinkle the layers with:

  1 cup shredded cheddar cheese

    __1__ cups cheddar

Beat until blended:

  2 eggs

    __6__ eggs

  2/3 cup milk

    __2__ cups milk

  1/4 teaspoon salt

    __3/4__ teaspoon salt

  1/8 teaspoon paprika

    __3/8 (1/4)__ teaspoon paprika

Pour this mixture over the macaroni. Sprinkle the top with:

Au Gratin

  3 slices dry bread

    __3__ slices bread

  2 tablespoons butter

    __2__ tablespoons butter

  1/3 cup cheddar cheese

    __1/3__ cup cheddar

Put bread in the blender to make fine bread crumbs. Sprinkle over macaroni mixture, dot with butter, and sprinkle with cheddar cheese. Bake about 40 minutes.

66

Answers

Integrating Academics

Let's Make Cookies

We need eight dozen cookies for the bake sale on Saturday. Our recipe only makes 36 cookies. Adjust the amounts on the following recipe so that you will have enough for the sale and one extra dozen for you and your friend to sample. (For example: If we needed six dozen, we would multiply by two.)

Chocolate Chip Drop Cookies
Makes 36 cookies
Preheat oven to 375°.

Multiply each amount by 2.

Cream:

    1/2 cup butter   ___1___ cups butter

    1/2 cup brown sugar   ___1___ cups sugar

    1/2 cup white sugar   ___1___ cups sugar

Beat in:

    1 egg   ___2___ eggs

    1/2 teaspoon vanilla   ___1___ teaspoons vanilla

Sift and stir in:

    1 cup plus 2 tablespoons flour   ___2-1/4___ cups flour

    1/3 teaspoon salt   ___2/3___ teaspoon salt

    1/2 teaspoon baking soda   ___1___ teaspoons baking soda

Stir in:

    3/4 cup chocolate chips   ___1-1/2___ cups chocolate chips

    1/2 cup chopped nuts   ___1___ cups chopped nuts

Drop the batter from a teaspoon, well apart, on a greased cookie sheet. Bake about 10 minutes.

68

Math

Name _____ Date _____ Period _____

Integrating Academics

Lasagna

Lasagna is a favorite food of most teenagers. It is easily prepared and can be made ahead of time from ingredients readily available. We want to plan a lunch with lasagna as the main dish. You and three friends will be eating. The recipe we have serves 16 people. Reduce the recipe to serve four.

Quick Lasagna (serves 16)   **4 servings**

Quick Lasagna (serves 16)	4 servings	
1 32 oz. jar of prepared Italian meat sauce	*8 oz.*	*Each amount needs to be divided by 4.*
2 lb. ricotta cheese	*1/2 lb.*	
1 lb. crumbled mozzarella cheese	*1/4 lb.*	
2 cups grated Parmesan cheese	*1/2 cup*	
1 lb. lasagna noodles	*1/4 lb.*	

Math

1. Boil the noodles in a large saucepan of water with 2 tablespoons olive oil. Stir to keep the noodles separate. Cook to *al dente* (somewhat firm; not too soft) stage; drain.

2. Preheat oven to 350 degrees.

3. Spread a thin layer of sauce on the bottom of a small baking dish. Layer the noodles and cheeses and the rest of the sauce saving enough Parmesan cheese to sprinkle on the top.

4. Bake about 30 to 40 minutes. Let stand briefly before cutting and serving.

What other dishes would be appropriate to serve with the lasagna? Write your menu below.

Menu

71

Name _____ Date _____ Period _____

Integrating Academics

Food Tips

Today, nearly one third of all meals consumed are eaten out. Some of the meals may be from "fast-food" restaurants. These restaurants offer fast service by which you order at a line and bring your food to the table yourself. Other restaurants, in which you are seated at a table and waited on by waiters and waitresses, offer a more leisurely service. The servers who wait on you receive a small salary, but usually a "tip" is the largest part of their pay. If you think the service is good, your tip should be between 15 and 20 percent of the bill. You should always check your bill to be sure it is correct.

1. Add the total bill of each of the restaurant checks below.

2. Determine the correct sales tax for your state.

3. Calculate a fifteen percent tip on each of the checks.

Guest Check	
Green salad	4.50
Roast beef	11.50
Coffee	1.00
Lemon pie	3.75
Total	20.75
Sales tax	1.25
	.06 (depends on state)
Tip	3.11
	(.15 x 20.75)
Total	25.10

Guest Check	
Tomato-dill soup	4.35
Lemon chicken	9.45
Iced tea	1.00
Carrrot cake	3.55
Total	18.35
Sales tax	1.10
	.06 (depends on state)
Tip	2.75
	(.15 x 18.35)
Total	22.20

77

Name _____ Date _____ Period _____

Integrating Academics

Floor Covering

One of the most dramatic ways of changing the decor of a room is to change the floor covering. Sales are constantly advertised. Floor coverings are priced by the square yard, and room sizes are measured by square feet so a little math is required. Remember that to get the square footage of a room, the width is multiplied by the length. **Example:** if a room is 12 × 18, the square feet are 216. To calculate the number of square yards 216 is divided by 9. (There are 3 feet in one yard.)

Calculate the number of square yards in the following rooms. Then find the cost of re-covering the floor at the price given per square yard.

Room # 1 10 × 16
Covering is $12.99 per square yard

10 x 16 = 160 sq. ft.

160 ÷ 9 = 17.77 sq. yds.

$12.99 x 17.77 = $230.93

$230.93
x .06 sales tax
$13.85
+ $230.93

Cost _____ $244.78 _____

Room # 2 12 × 24
Covering is $16.99 per square yard.

12 x 24 = 288 sq. ft.

288 ÷ 9 = 32 sq. yds.

$16.99 x 32 = $543.68

$543.68
x .06 sales tax
$32.62
+ $543.68

Cost _____ $576.30 _____

Room # 3 9 × 13
Covering is $24.99 per square yard

9 x 13 = 117 sq. ft.

117 ÷ 9 = 13 sq. yds.

$24.99 x 13 = $324.87

$324.87
x .06 sales tax
$19.49
+ $324.87

Cost _____ $344.36 _____

98

Math

Name _____ Date _____ Period _____

Integrating Academics

Wallpapering

Many do-it-yourself projects around the house are fun, easy, and can save money for the person brave enough to learn the process. One method of changing a room decor is to cover the walls with paper, cloth, or vinyl wallcoverings. Wallpapers are sold in rolls. A single roll will cover 30 square feet.

To estimate the number of rolls needed:

1. Measure the distance around the room (including door openings).

2. Measure the height of the ceiling.

3. Multiply the ceiling height by the distance around the room (round off to the nearest foot) and divide by 30. From this number, subtract 1/2 roll for each regular size window and door.

The result (rounded to the next whole number) is the number of single rolls you need to cover the entire room.

Example: A room is 10 feet wide and 12 feet long with a ceiling height of 8 feet.

$2 \times 10 = 20$
$2 \times 12 = \underline{24}$
$\qquad 44 \times 8 = 352 \div 30 = \qquad 11.73$ rolls
There is one window and one door − $\underline{\quad 1.00}$
$\qquad\qquad\qquad\qquad\qquad\qquad 10.73$ rolls rounded to 11 rolls.

Calculate the number of rolls of wallpaper needed to paper a room with these proportions.

width—14 feet
length—18 feet
height—8 feet
There are 2 windows and 1 door.

$2 \times 14 = 28$
$2 \times 18 = \underline{36}$
$\qquad 64 \times 8 = 512$ ft.

windows — 1   roll
$\quad$ door — 1/2 roll
$\qquad \overline{1\,1/2}$ (subtract only 1 roll, you cannot buy 1/2 roll)

$512 \div 30 = \quad 17$ rolls
$\qquad\qquad\qquad \underline{-1}$
$\qquad\qquad\qquad\quad 16$

Number of rolls needed __16__

99

Math

Name _____ Date _____ Period _____

Integrating Academics

Buying a House

The American dream almost always includes a home of one's own. Because very few people have the money to pay cash for a house, a mortgage is usually required. There are certain guidelines used by lending institutions which have been designed to keep families from getting into financial difficulties later on. These guidelines not only consider a family income but whether a couple has dependants. Single people can usually afford to pay proportionately more of their income toward the purchase of a home than a family with children.

Single persons or married couples with no children are allowed up to **33%** of their gross monthly income as the limit for a house payment. This amount should include the principal, interest, property taxes, and homeowners' insurance.

A couple with children should not exceed **28%** of their gross monthly income for the house payment.

Calculate the payments which the families below could make using these guidelines.

1. The Ruiz family consists of a mother with three children. Her income from a job as a physician is $94,000 a year.

    .28 x $94,000 ÷12 = $2,193.33 per month

    Payment <u>$2,193.33</u>

2. Joe and Linda Smith have combined incomes of $42,000. Their children are grown and do not live at home.

    .33 x $42,000 ÷12 = $1,155 per month

    Payment <u>$1,155</u>

3. Brenda and Mike have four children. She does not work, and Mike makes $38,000 a year as a teacher.

    .28 x $38,000 ÷12 = $886.66 per month

    Payment <u>$886.66</u>

104

Math

Name _____ Date _____ Period _____

Integrating Academics

Real Estate Terminology

Refer to the list of terms below to fill in the blanks of this home-buying case study. If you do not know the meaning of the words, look them up in your textbook or a reference book in the library.

Mortgage	Title	Insurance	Sales comission
Closing cost	Real estate agent	Guarantee	Taxes
Termite	Taxes	Interest	
Credit	Appraiser	Deed	
Loan application	Down payment	Principal	

Chuck and Cindy decided that the safest way to buy their first house was to find a good

_____real estate agent_____. Once they started looking, they did not take long to find the perfect

house. They decided to limit their price range so the payment would not exceed 25% of their

income. They went to a lending institution to fill out a _____loan application_____. They found

they could _____guarantee_____ a loan rate at closing if they paid a fee. Soon they discoved

other costs. The house 's value would have to be determined by an _____appraiser_____.

Their _____credit_____ would have to be checked for financial stability. They decided to

pay 20% _____down payment_____ to lower the amount of money they needed to borrow. The

_____sales commission_____ they paid their real estate agent was a good investment. She arranged

for a _____termite_____ inspection and builiding inspection. She also contacted the real

estate attorney to handle the _____title_____ search and to see that the

_____deed_____ was recorded at the courthouse. They discovered that some of the

_____taxes_____ would have to be prorated and that homeowners'

_____insurance_____ was required by the lending institution. Their house payment would

include _____principal_____, _____interest_____, _____taxes_____ and insur-

ance. When the day arrived for closing they had all their papers in order and checks written to

pay the _____closing cost_____. They now had a home and a _____mortgage_____ which

they would pay on for 30 years.

114

Language Arts